Motherlode

Life Writing Series

In the Life Writing Series, Wilfrid Laurier University Press publishes life writing and new life-writing criticism and theory in order to promote autobiographical accounts, diaries, letters, and testimonials written and/or told by women and men whose political, literary, or philosophical purposes are central to their lives. The Series features accounts written in English, or translated into English from French or the languages of the First Nations, or any of the languages of immigration to Canada.

From its inception, Life Writing has aimed to foreground the stories of those who may never have imagined themselves as writers or as people with lives worthy of being (re)told. Its readership has expanded to include scholars, youth, and avid general readers both in Canada and abroad. The Series hopes to continue its work as a leading publisher of life writing of all kinds, as an imprint that aims for both broad representation and scholarly excellence, and as a tool for both historical and autobiographical research.

As its mandate stipulates, the Series privileges those individuals and communities whose stories may not, under normal circumstances, find a welcoming home with a publisher. Life Writing also publishes original theoretical investigations about life writing, as long as they are not limited to one author or text.

Series Editor
Marlene Kadar
Humanities Division, York University

Manuscripts to be sent to
Lisa Quinn, Acquisitions Editor
Wilfrid Laurier University Press
75 University Avenue West
Waterloo, Ontario N2L 3C5
Canada

Motherlode

A Mosaic of Dutch Wartime Experience

Carolyne Van Der Meer

WILFRID LAURIER
UNIVERSITY PRESS

Wilfrid Laurier University Press acknowledges the support of the Canada Council for the Arts for our publishing program. We acknowledge the financial support of the Government of Canada through the Canada Book Fund for our publishing activities.

Library and Archives Canada Cataloguing in Publication

Van Der Meer, Carolyne A., 1968–, author
　　Motherlode : a mosaic of Dutch wartime experience / Carolyne Van Der Meer.

(Life writing series)
Issued in print and electronic formats.
ISBN 978-1-77112-005-0 (pbk.).—ISBN 978-1-77112-006-7 (pdf).—ISBN 978-1-77112-007-4 (epub)

　　1. Van Der Meer, Carolyne A., 1968– —Family—Literary collections. 2. Netherlands—History—German occupation, 1940–1945—Literary collections. 3. World War, 1939–1945—Personal narratives, Dutch—Literary collections. I. Title. II. Series: Life writing series

PS8643.A5265M68 2014　　C818'.6　　C2013-905894-X　　C2013-905895-8

Cover design by Sandra Friesen. Front-cover photo: The author's mother's childhood home (middle) in the village of De Krim, Overijssel, 1943. Text design by Sandra Friesen.

© 2014 Wilfrid Laurier University Press
Waterloo, Ontario, Canada
www.wlupress.wlu.ca

This book is printed on FSC® recycled paper and is certified Ecologo. It is made from 100% post-consumer fibre, processed chlorine free, and manufactured using biogas energy.

Printed in Canada

Every reasonable effort has been made to acquire permission for copyright material used in this text, and to acknowledge all such indebtedness accurately. Any errors and omissions called to the publisher's attention will be corrected in future printings.

For my mother, Wilma Van Der Meer (née Wietske Smallegange)

And for Robert and Eric

Contents

4: The Fighters

Preface

This collection of poems, short stories, and essays was initially inspired by stories I'd heard as a young girl about my mother's childhood in Nazi-occupied Holland. But the book you now hold, *Motherlode: A Mosaic of Dutch Wartime Experience*, grew into much more as I wrote it, and now examines the Dutch experience during the occupation from myriad perspectives, thanks to the generous collaboration of several other individuals.

I began with the goal of preserving my mother's family legacy—a legacy of helping Jews, including by hiding them from their persecutors, and of resistance work that helped to undermine German rule. But what I discovered during my research was the everyday hardship of war, and the emotions that went with it—the hopelessness and the hope, the terror and the joy, the inner wealth and the outer poverty. This collection is not so much about history as about feeling.

It all began with my mother's letters. Late one night, I made a long-distance call to her home in Belleville, Ontario, and asked her to write down everything she could remember about growing up in Holland during the war. Born in De Krim, Overijssel, about five kilometres from the German border, she was two years old when Holland surrendered, and says of the war, "It was all I knew." This was our starting point. It was hard for her. Her brothers had already asked her to tell these stories in detail, but she had refused. Then when I told her about my plan to write a book, she agreed to help me, and I am forever indebted to her for that. Her willingness took our relationship down a new road.

When I visited her childhood village in the summer of 2010, I had no difficulty locating her old house along the canal—a house whose image has long been etched into my memory thanks to faded, dog-eared photos. And good fortune was with me that day: the owners were home and one of them, Canadian-born Gordon van Wezel, spoke fluent English. As I stood in the backyard, I was finally able to imagine—*really imagine*—what it might have been like for my mother to run in mad fright during an air raid when she should have dropped to the ground and stayed still. During my tour of the house, I studied the ceiling, looking for the false floor between the first and second storeys where Jewish families were once hidden.

And so the first section of this volume is dedicated to my mother and her past, as well as to the journey we made together as we reflected on this time in her life. The essay "The Complexity of Belonging" examines the questions of heritage, legacy, and belonging that I faced along the way.

When I realized that my mother's memories were too limited for me to complete an entire manuscript, I began to consider other avenues. This led to the writing of three further sections: "The Children," "The Survivors," and "The Fighters." But this was the result of several steps. First, I contacted University of Calgary professor Dr. Herman Ganzevoort, who has written articles and books about post–World War II Dutch emigration to Canada. At Dr. Ganzevoort's suggestion, I contacted the Canadian Association for the Advancement of Netherlandic Studies, where my efforts were rewarded. The president of the Montreal chapter at the time, Peter Lowensteyn, emailed my request for information about those years to his entire membership. For several weeks, responses came in steadily from Dutch immigrants of my mother's generation who were willing to talk about their experiences. Interviews with Libby Boelen Emond, Carla Stapensea, and Kees Vanderheyden have added another dimension to this collection. Their stories have inspired poems and short stories that help illustrate the Dutch experience from various perspectives.

My 2010 trip to the Netherlands yielded more material. I spent hours at the Netherlands Institute for War Documentation and the Jewish Historical Museum, both of which had excellent librarians who helped me discover *onderduik*,* the hiding period, from the Dutch perspective. These institutions

My mother's childhood home (second from left), seen from the other side of the
canal in 2010. Located on the village of De Krim's Hoofdweg, or "Main Street,"
it stands among other homes that have, like my mother's home, undergone
significant gentrification since 1943, when the cover photo was taken.

gave me a sense of what it was like for families to put their lives at risk for
those who were being persecuted. In addition, the Netherlands Institute
for War Documentation had a breadth of material on the Dutch resistance
movement. Between this and further research at the Dutch Resistance Museum, I began to feel comfortable with this project. I am indebted to all of
these institutions and their well-qualified staff.

This collection is a mix of fact and fiction. I wanted to capture the voices
of the time. And if I couldn't capture that immediacy, I wanted to harness
the power of memory in all its rawness. For this reason, I have, in many
places, used the very words of various subjects, closely adhering to the style of
Charles Reznikoff's "found poems." And in some cases, I have taken a single
nugget of truth and built an entire narrative around it. The pieces in this
volume are fictional reconstructions of real events that attempt to validate
and legitimize elements of the Dutch experience in an occupied nation, and
beyond. My mother provided the framework, but it became a collaborative
effort involving many people and their stories.

There are wonderful things that come out of undertaking a project of this nature. First, it has connected me with my roots. Second, it preserves and honours my mother's past, as well as the experiences of so many people who generously gave their time, including Libby, Carla, and Kees. Amsterdam shopkeeper Anna Massee provided information about her Dutch-resistance-worker grandparents, Charlotte Schouten Escher and Jan Willem Schouten. The stories of Canadian Jewish soldiers David Kucer and Ralph Rogow are also explored here, and their perspective on the liberation of Holland adds a crucial dimension to this collection. Dutch Jewish war refugee Nico Hamme, who escaped to Belgium during the occupation, told me his story, and Dutch-born Irish resident Pier Kuipers contributed a letter that his grandparents wrote during the liberation. I was fortunate enough to connect with all these individuals or, in some cases, their children. As a result of this project, I have become closer to my mother than I have ever been.

Prologue

The letter shakes between my fingers. I set it down on the counter and drop a tea bag into the cup as the kettle begins its impatient whistle. A brief flavouring of sugar and I pour the steaming water. The pages continue to beckon. It's from my mother, and hopefully it explores another chapter of her childhood during the war.

For months now, I've been asking her questions about her early years in Nazi-occupied Holland, mostly in letters containing long lists of queries, posted with impatience. And even when it's too soon to expect a response, I still check the mailbox daily. It's been an exercise that has drawn us much closer—my interest in her past has revalued those experiences for her. Indeed, I heard many versions of her stories as a child, but I didn't understand their importance as my legacy. I never really grasped their claim on me, or mine on them. Only now can I appreciate their significance and allow myself to be held by their power—yes, only now do I have the life experience I need to transform them into stories.

After creating a warmish tea with far too much milk, I take the letter in one hand, the cup in the other, and move towards the living-room sofa. Her letter is short, only two pages, but I hope to find something here—more magic, more evidence of who this woman was before she became my mother. *Before she became* just *my mother*, is the thought in my head, but I stop myself from thinking it. Indeed, suddenly she was rising from the pages as much more—as a whole being with hopes and dreams that had nothing to do with me or my siblings. How often do we think of our parents this way? I've only ever taken her for granted—as I suppose most children do. I've thought that she lives just for me, to take care of me—that those youthful desires were supplanted by my very existence. Who was she then? Now that I'm a mother too, I understand that thinking of her in this way is wrong—my own hopes and dreams have not died with the birth of my son. They are just prioritized differently. But it's only now that I'm really contemplating what she may have wanted and imagined.

Once I've settled in my spot on the sofa, I pick up the letter and begin to read. Her first sentence is devastating, not just because of what it actually says but because of what it implies—what it makes me realize. *"Nice of you to write, too bad there are always a bunch of questions that come with it. It's really ok, it is just that I can't make you understand."*

I feel a thud somewhere inside, like something has gone horribly wrong. And I hadn't had the intuitive power to understand it. I had thought that she was enjoying this exchange—this opportunity to share her long-buried inner world with me. I had viewed it as an opportunity, a rich one, but her words make me see that I'm wrong. And I can't decide whether she's angry with me or just exasperated. Does she mean that I'm too thick to get it, or is she questioning her own ability to express her thoughts and explain that part of her life to me? And, beyond my own insecurities, her words raise another issue: Am I asking too much of her? Does she not want to do this? And if she doesn't, why doesn't she just tell me?

But her words give me pause about the larger issue of memory. Conversations with other Dutch war children have made me see what I won't allow my mother—that these are terrifying memories and compassion is necessary. I need to realize that she has blocked it out, and that it has taken quite a focused effort to do so. She grew up with the sounds of war in her ears and worked hard to forget them, to overwrite them with new, better sounds. I find the unearthing of her memories fascinating—arresting. But for her, it is like the sting of pulling off a well-stuck Band-Aid. I'm undoing her, and now I wonder if it's unfair to bring her back to such a vulnerable place.

1940: My mother at the age of two, with her older brother, Johan. This photo was probably taken just after the Nazi occupation began.

Despite my unsettled feeling, I read the rest of her letter with the same hunger I had read the other letters with. She answered my questions systematically, with surprisingly good sentence structure. Here and there, she had circled and underlined words, as she usually does when she's unsure of their spelling. I smile, imagining her furrowed brow as she draws round and round these words, the pen pressing deep lines into the paper. Of course I know I have to call her. I turn her letter over again and reread it, briefly procrastinating. Taking a last sip of my tea, I get up, take the cup to the kitchen, and pick up the phone.

She answers on the second ring.

"Hi Mom," I say.

"Hi, Carolyne. How are you? Did you get my letter?" she asks, her words rapidly flooding the line.

"I did," I say. "Just now. That's why I'm calling you." I pause. "I'm so sorry this is upsetting you, Mom. You should have told me."

"It's not just that," she tells me. "It's that I can't seem to explain it properly. You keep asking me the same questions."

I explain that sometimes I'm focusing on a different detail, trying to force her memory to retrieve some bit that seems important to me—something

1942: My mother (left) with her brothers Johan, Theo, and Albert, all of whom are now deceased.

that begs exploration. I remind her that I'm a journalist, and that it's all about getting the *whole* story. She tells me she understands and says she's sorry.

"It's hard," she says. "It's hard to go back and think about all these things. I've tried so hard to forget."

"Do you want to stop?" I ask her. "I don't want you to do this if it upsets you."

"No," she says. "I said I would, and I'm going to. You're the only person I'll do it for. My brothers have often asked me about our childhood and I've refused. But I will do it for you."

She's an emotional person, particularly as she gets older, but at this moment, her voice is strong. She means what she says. And I hear a smile come down the line. "But don't let it take too long," she adds.

I laugh and promise her that I'll do my best.

Our discussion makes me question the facts of memory: How things get buried and are left to rot until someone, or something, disturbs them. How our memories are selective. How we lock the painful images away and live our lives as though certain events have not happened, even though they have shaped us. We all do it. Compartmentalize. Lock things away in a drawer. And my mother has agreed to open the drawer, the proverbial Pandora's box:

memories—images and sounds—that shake her to her core. That bring her to a place she never wants to go again.

What she has given me, though, is more than we both realized. For her, it's a drawer she is opening at will. But for me, it's a key. A key to who she is—and, ultimately, to who I am. It's a cultural inheritance—something that has always been mine but that I have been ignorant of until now. And now that I'm aware of this inheritance, I can understand its richness and share it.

Chapter One

Finding the Motherlode

18 July 2010

It's 6:10 p.m. My flight boards at 7 p.m. I've been waiting all my adult life to make this trip. I think about all that's bound up in it: understanding the past, where I came from, my mother, and what she lived through—in wartime and after. I want to see where she grew up, and associate the stories she has told me with places I see with my own eyes.

Going Home

I am strapped in, no room to move
on this transatlantic flight
Were they
like this, constricted between the floorboards,
barely daring to draw a breath? My mother hid
in her mama's skirts, the SS officer demanding a
search in the folds of night. I feel the aircraft lurch,
turbulence
then and now

Parched

Gate B1
I sit, breathe
drink
soon I will arrive
quench other thirst
trace winding roots
of childhood stories
uniformed SS
coming to the window
demanding water
thanking you as you
looked skittishly at
loose floorboards, like
the ones upstairs, under
which you hid *Joden**
I have come to find the
floorboards, look
as you looked
more than sixty years
ago

19 July 2010

It's ten o'clock in the morning, and I'm at Frankfurt Airport. I walk through the shops to get a sense of what things cost as I wait for a gate to be assigned to my flight. I find a reclining chair near a departures board and wait. The chair wobbles and I wonder if the movement is meant to mimic rocking, designed to calm the weary traveller. It's not working—there is only a feeling of discombobulation.

Finally, the gate is assigned—A28—and my first panic about where to go subsides. I'm nervous about what awaits me—what I will find and what I might not find. Will this trip help fill in the blanks about my mother's life? Give me insight into her world—and maybe into me?

My stomach hurts, and my eyes are swollen from lack of sleep. I've removed my contacts and I'm wearing glasses. The last thing I feel is hunger. I know it's four o'clock in the morning, but I've eaten supper and then breakfast and it's bright outside, so my body really believes it's ten o'clock in the morning. I feel completely dislocated, suspended. This must be how Robert, my husband, feels when business travel dominates his life: lost hours of nothingness suspended in flight. It's like you're in a vacuum, the time–space continuum interrupted, a chunk that's forever out of reach.

Who am I, here in Frankfurt? Some girl with glasses, sitting on a bench. No identity. My few possessions in two bags linked around my wrist. Travelling is lonely. Like you've lost the connection with what you know and love. There's no frame of reference. You're hanging. This must be what Mom felt like when she arrived in Canada after the war. She needed to "become." And now I need to figure out who she was before that so I can do the same.

My thoughts jump to Robert again, and the fact that I've never really thought about what he feels when he's away from us. I just know he's not where I am, which is the overwhelming sensation. I have no concept of that singular world in which he resides as he gets from one place to the next. I can see how, for a moment, you might think you're someone else, wonder where it all went. What if you could never find it again?

It will be good to arrive in Amsterdam, have a shower, ease off that suspension in never-never land. When I get to the hotel, I'll have a base camp, and that awful feeling of being stuck will go.

I spend the afternoon in the west quarter, walking through the Jordaan,* full of bohemian storefronts and coffee houses. The odours of pot and hash are heavy— you can get a buzz passing through. I walk down the Haarlemmerstraat* and cut down the Prinsengracht,* all the way to the Westerkerk* near the Anne Frank House. It's late in the day and the church is closed. The lineup at the Anne Frank House winds around the corner of the building. I go to the Amsterdam Tulip Museum instead, which is bright and cheerful, and small enough to take in despite my fatigue. There are lovely things in the shop—the Dutch like simple lines and fine quality. I walk back up the Prinsengracht and find a shop filled wall-to-wall with Delft Blue pieces, many for exorbitant sums. Mom loves this stuff; she'd be in heaven.

I've been here only a few hours and it feels right. Like I belong. What's odd is that Mom and her 1940s Dutch culture are so removed from this. She'd be intimidated in her own country, with drugs, pickpocketing, and prostitution in plain sight. She is truly dislocated—she would lose her north if she came back. Just as Nancy Huston writes in her collection of essays Losing North, *in choosing a new land and giving yourself over to it, you lose touch with your homeland. It's something you never quite get back. And even though you're not of the new land, you've chosen it, and that makes it home. And then, ironically, your homeland becomes the lost north.*

Letters from a War Child

The letters are like a run-on sentence:
words, emotions,
spilling from my mother
as though they will get away from her
if she doesn't hurry. She glosses
over the ugly parts of the war, claiming
a faulty memory
but remembers with candid
detail the things that brought her
joy:
flowers in her small garden
her father's aviary
homegrown honey—
the fairy-story elements of her young life.
Today she only watches movies with
happy endings, reads romance novels that turn
out right.
No war films or documentaries.
The hiss-bang of
dropping bombs,
the frantic pitch of air-raid sirens
send her diving
for cover. I wonder at this denial,
chase her sentences
as they run underground,
mine them for all that
got left behind, for all that
she does not want to find.

Nine Ways to Happiness in Wartime

Plant a garden
Occupied rule can't deprive me of
asters, daisies, marigolds, and dahlias
Give flowers in bunches
Sometimes I bring them to Mama. It
makes her smile
Eat fresh peaches
Wild, no bigger than plums,
their fuzz is softer than anything I know
Harvest your own vegetables
We dig them up, store them in dirt
on a bed of straw, just enough to get through winter
Make cherry preserves
Sour cherries jubilee in jars
I dream of eating ice cream again one day
Hide your radio
Sure misery if they confiscate it
we wrap it in a blanket so it doesn't rattle, hide it under floorboards
Be nice to the soldiers
Most of them don't mean you harm;
besides, the price of rudeness is too high
Watch who you talk to
Those NSB'ers,* our beloved fellow Dutchmen,
are everywhere
Hold your head high
What else can you do?
Hope.

Marijke's Song

Marijke jumped out of bed. It was finally here—the day she would spend in the shop with Papa. She'd been looking forward to this for weeks, never quite knowing when it would happen since he was away so much. She rushed through her breakfast of bread soaked in milk and bounded into the shoe-making studio.

"Slow down!" her mother called after her. "You'll trip if you're not careful!" It didn't clip her wings one bit.

She stood by her father's side in the shop workroom, barely able to contain her excitement. She watched as he slipped his large index finger under the sole of the shoe, already partially separated from the leather upper, and pulled. It gave, leaving the husk in his hand. It was dirty, but she knew he could work his magic and make a shoe almost as good as new with another sole and some polish. He finally looked up from his work and smiled.

"Now, Marijke, do you want to help Papa today?" She'd been waiting for him to ask her. She loved working in the shop, either giving out the repaired shoes in their thick brown paper wrapping, or handing him pieces of leather and spools of thread as he made repairs and crafted new footwear. At five, she wasn't old enough to do much on her own, but she knew she made a good little helper. As Papa playfully touched the end of her nose with his finger, the strong smell of rawhide stung her nostrils. It was a smell she loved, one that made her think of him and him alone.

He'd been back for two weeks now and Marijke couldn't get enough of him. Every morning when she woke up and remembered he was home, her heart felt too big for her chest. She dreaded him leaving again. Last time he was gone for five weeks and it had seemed like forever. She knew he worked for the Resistance but she didn't really understand what that was or what he did. Secret things. Dangerous things. A part of her worried about him, another part made him into a spy hero, a man who was never frightened and was always courageous.

"I always want to help, Papa. What can I do today?"

"How about serving the customers? A number of people have promised to pick up their repairs today," he said.

Nodding her head, she slipped her small fingers into his huge palm. With his free hand, he ruffled her golden locks and led her out of the workroom to the storefront. Behind the counter, they began to organize the bags. He stacked them in an armoire, thick brown paper packages that Marijke liked the feel of, not like the thin stuff she used for making drawings at home. When he asked, she put out her arms, wanting desperately to be useful. Trying to make space in the armoire, Papa removed several packages and placed them on her outstretched arms. She was glad he gave her the lighter ones so that she could manage them. Two, three, four bags and she began to stagger.

"Okay, Marijke, just hold those," he said, and pushed several bags towards the back of the shelf, placing them one atop the other instead of leaving them askew, then taking the bags from Marijke one by one and putting them at the front. "There. Now we're ready," he said with a frown. She knew he must be thinking about money. But she'd also seen soldiers come and take all the money. She guessed this must be worrying him.

"Do you think anyone will show up, Papa?" Marijke asked.

"We'll see," he said. He sat on the only stool and gently pulled his daughter onto his lap. She loved sitting there, so high that she could see over the countertop without having to balance on the tips of her toes. She hadn't felt this happy in so long, having her father home and being able to spend time alone with him while her mother worked with her brothers in the back garden.

The clanging of the bell and the whap-whap of the door hitting the frame brought Marijke from her reverie. Papa rose from the stool, lifting her and setting her squarely on the floor.

"Hello, Wim," a tall man said, placing his yellow claim slip on the counter.

"*Guten morgen*, Kees," Papa said, taking the slip and handing it to Marijke. She thought the man looked familiar but couldn't be sure. "How are things in Coevorden?" she heard Papa ask as she went to find the boots. She took a quick look at this man Kees and didn't like what she saw—a reddish face, a mess of straw-coloured hair, and a veiny nose that looked like it had a big ball on the end of it. She stuck her head into the armoire, all the while straining to hear everything they said. She had noticed right away that Papa was acting strangely. He seemed nervous. She wondered if it had something to do with his being away so much. She had often heard the soldiers asking where he was and why he wasn't at home.

"I've been busy trying to deal with a census exercise. You know, figuring out who is living where," Kees said, pausing. "It's a bad business," he added, rubbing the wrinkled space between his eyes.

Marijke wondered why it mattered who lived where, but she knew better than to ask. She thought about those people who would come to stay sometimes—the ones with the yellow stars on their coats—and how they couldn't tell anyone they were there.

"Yes, it's a bad business," her father replied. She peeked around the armoire door and saw his lips become thin, just like when he was about to get cross with her. He looked as though he wanted to say something, but he kept quiet.

Marijke's head and most of her small body were buried in the armoire, and, as she listened, she carefully turned over each tag to check the number against the yellow paper. It was just as well she had her back turned; she didn't like the man's skin, which looked like it had little holes in it, or his watery eyes. The odd thing was, he didn't look much like he was about to cry.

She had seen Papa stiffen when they were talking about the "bad business." Marijke wasn't sure what it was all about, but she wanted her father to know she was on his side. While she hunted for the boots, she thought about what she could do. And then, just as she put her small hands on the right package, it came to her. Slowly, almost inaudibly at first, she began to hum. It was that song they all sang, the one about the traitors Mama and Papa hated—what were they called again? Oh, yes. The NSB'ers. The ones who helped the Nazis.

As she fumbled in the armoire, she began to feel more confident about singing and the words came out involuntarily:

Op de hoek van de straat
Staat een NSB'er
't is geen man, 't is geen vrouw
Maar een Farizeeër
Met een krant in z'n hand
Staat hij daar te venten
Hij verkoopt zijn vaderland
Voor wat losse centen.

At the street corner
Stands an NSB'er
It's not a man, it's not a woman
But a Pharisee

With the paper in his hand
He stands there to sell
He sells his fatherland
For a few loose cents.

She wasn't even sure what a Pharisee was, but she knew it had something to do with Jesus and Judas. She felt proud in that instant, thinking that Papa would be pleased she remembered her Bible lessons. As she came to the end of the chorus, her voice reached the highest, richest note, the part she liked best. But before she could rejoice further in her performance, one of the armoire doors came crashing closed, and she saw her father's face a few inches from her own, twisted in a way she had never seen before. As the colour drained from Marijke's cheeks, he snatched the paper bag from her and turned to Kees once more.

"You'll have to excuse my daughter," he said, handing the package to his customer with a suddenly calm voice. "The things kids hear in the street," he added, looking apologetic.

Marijke saw the man give her father an odd look—almost angry, but not quite. Then he laughed hard and loud. "You should hear what my kids bring home!" After handing him some coins, Kees shook Papa's hand as though everything was normal. They said goodbye and he left the shop.

Marijke cowered behind her father. He turned swiftly towards her once the door had clicked shut.

"Papa, I'm—" she began, but he cut her off.

"Get upstairs, Marijke! NOW!" he roared. "And stay OUT of my sight!" As Marijke turned, her tiny skirt clinging to woollen tights, she felt him grab her shoulders. He raised his knee and pushed it into her backside. She stumbled forward as he released her. Hot humiliation raced up her neck, staining her cheeks red as she took the stairs two at a time. When she reached the top, she tripped, smashing her nose against the door. The sting spread over her face and into her eyes, drawing salty tears. Feeling the trickle of blood in one nostril, she moved the back of her hand up quickly to catch it and smeared a mixture of snot and crimson across her cheek. She fumbled with the latch, stepped quickly into their living quarters, and closed the door softly behind her, breathing hard.

The sound of cutlery clattering in the sink and her mother's voice cut into her thoughts. "Marijke? What on earth ...?" Hennie began, stopping in the doorway between the kitchen and the sitting room. Kneeling with arms outstretched, she called softly to her daughter. "Come here and tell me what happened."

"Mama," Marijke whimpered as she stepped forward. "Mama, I sang the song in front of that man Kees from Coevorden. You know, the Pharisee song. And Papa got so angry. What did I do wrong? I thought it was funny. I thought everyone liked that funny song."

"Oh, Marijke," Hennie said, stroking her daughter's fine blond hair. "Singing that song is like saying what side you're on. You can't do that unless you know what side the other person is on."

Marijke put her arms around her mother's neck and began to sob. "I didn't know, Mama, I didn't know." She felt her mother pick her up and carry her to the bathroom.

"It's okay, child. He'll get over it." As Mama wiped the blood from her nose, Marijke realized what this might mean—that Papa would disappear again, maybe for longer than ever before. She cried even harder, wishing she could take it all back—the song, everything.

20 July 2010

It's nine thirty in the morning, and I'm sitting in the New Dorrius, the hotel restaurant, eating a traditional Dutch breakfast: heavy grain bread, thin-sliced ham and chicken, havarti, and Gouda. Also roggebrood, the dense pumpernickel bread that Mom ate as a child—and now can't stand. The apricots are soaked in marinade and I wonder if I can bring some home.

I realize, as my tea gets cold, that the research for this book is providing me with a unique opportunity to understand my mother, to get closer to her in the later years of her life. When I think of her as a little girl growing up in wartime, surrounded by German soldiers, steeped in poverty, and living in fear of air raids, my reaction is physical. I shudder, and think of how terrified my grandmother must have been for her brood, ever growing in an age of no birth control.

I finish my tea, gather my things, and head back to my room to freshen up. I'm meeting my friend Kate in an hour. It's time to switch gears.

❦

Kate and I find each other in the hotel lobby at ten thirty. We've known each other for nearly five years—were connected by a friend through email—but this is the first time we've met face to face. Many letters and packages have passed in the mail in the last few years, and Kate and I have come to know each other well. What had drawn us together was the odd coincidence that she lives in the same suburb of Rotterdam where my father grew up. This led to many conversations, and she has been a constant resource for me during the writing of this book.

Our first stop is the Nieuwe Kerk, one of the most ornate Catholic churches in all of Amsterdam. It's no longer used for religious services—exhibitions and events are held here now. It's magnificent, with a floor-to-ceiling organ that dominates every viewpoint. Across the street is the Magna Plaza, a shopping centre filled with haute couture and, strangely, a disproportionate number of Montreal designers.

We go back to the square, around which are the church, the palace, and De Bijenkorf, the largest department store in Amsterdam, which is located on Dam Square, at the mouth of the shopping district, the Kalverstraat. We wander, somewhat disoriented, into the red-light district, where truly stunning women stand at their windows in G-strings and skimpy bras, oozing sex. Kate and I are surprised at their beauty. We expect used-up, disillusioned girls who no longer cared for themselves. Instead, we see young, pert bodies that tempt us both to see prostitution differently.

After a brief walk through these narrow streets, we find a canal-side café, where we order white beer and "warm geitje," which Kate translates as "warm goat," a clever name for goat cheese melted on that rich dark Dutch bread. As we drink our beer, she reminds me of our post-lunch destination: the Hollandsche Schouwburg, * a theatre that the Nazis transformed into a deportation centre for Jews being sent to transit camps like Westerbork in Drenthe or Vught in North Brabant. From Westerbork, Jews were sent on to Auschwitz for extermination. Vught was an SS camp for both Jews and political activists, and prisoners were classified before being sent on to camps in Poland and elsewhere. Kate tells me she came to the Hollandsche Schouwburg some twenty years ago and it haunts her still.

We finish lunch and pay, then begin our trek to the southeastern part of the city, through the Amsterdam Business School, with myriad detours, as Kate's sense of direction is worse than mine. We walk down Plantage Kerklaan and she stands on street corners, struggling to remember where the old theatre might be. At the end of the street is the popular Artis Royal Zoo, and just across from it, the Dutch Resistance Museum (Verzetsmuseum), where we stop to buy a book about the resistance movement. I make a note to come back tomorrow. When I pay, I tell the museum attendant we've been looking for the Hollandsche Schouwburg, and she laughs, tells us it's just around the corner. "Take a right at the next inter-section, onto Plantage Middenlaan," she tells us, "and you'll see a white, austere building on the other side of the street."

We find it with ease, chuckle at how close it was all along. When we enter, it feels like a shrine, a place where silence must be kept. The first-floor exhibit, en-titled "Persecution of the Jews, 1940–1945," is elaborate and all in Dutch. Kate takes me through, roughly translating the foreign words for me. There are two sections, one on persecution and one on resistance, which shares some common ground with the resistance movement initiated by the Dutch. The second floor is an education centre, which we look at quickly before heading back down to the monuments on the first floor and outdoors. But for Kate's whispered transla-tions, we are quiet.

Kate (left) and I in the Café Américain at the Amsterdam American Hotel.

We stand in front of the "wall of names," with all 6,700 family names of the 104,000 Dutch Jews who were murdered during the Nazi occupation. I think about the Jews my mother's family hid, and wonder how many of them survived.

We go to the outdoor theatre, a memorial chapel where an eternal flame burns. There are simple concrete benches with a tall obelisk standing at centre stage. The brick walls of the original theatre stand exposed to the elements. We sit in the first row, looking up at the structure for a long while.

We leave, neither of us saying much, and catch a tram for the Van Gogh Museum. Kate has purchased tickets for us—an early birthday gift for me, she says. The canvases lighten our mood; we are carried off by Van Gogh's dramatic brush strokes. Afterwards, we walk through the museum district and end up at the fountain in Leidse Square. In front of it is the popular Amsterdam American Hotel with its Café Americain, where writers are known to gather. Kate insists we stop at the outdoor bar and have a glass of wine and some Dutch finger foods: bitterballen, *a savoury, meat-based snack typically containing a mixture of beef, beef broth, flour and butter for thickening, parsley, and salt and pepper; spring-roll-like snacks called* vlammetjes, *or "little flames"; and* croquettes, *a* meat-based snack with a deep-fried dough exterior. We are both giddy from wine and emotion. Our waiter takes a photo of us, and months later, when I look at it, I will be able to recapture the sense of deep satisfaction brought by the day, of seeing an old friend and connecting on so many levels. It isn't just about our shared profession as writers. It's about our shared "Dutchness," and her belief in my writing project. And the complicit silence between us as we sat in front of the monument at the Hollandsche Schouwburg.

Later that evening, I sit in the hotel bar with a glass of shiraz, poring over my mom's letters. I'm trying to write a story about her interest in gardening getting her through the war, but I need to do some research on flowers before I can finish it. I consider starting another—about the family friend who worked with my grandfather in the Resistance, who was shot by the Nazis as he climbed the fence between their houses. But that needs research, too. I forgo the formal writing and contemplate the day.

The Poem about Hiding Jews

He comes up to me after my reading.
Slightly bearded, grey whiskers
poking on cleft chin, stark
blue eyes looking through me.
*What your family did during the
war*, he says, *was extraordinary.*
They are "righteous gentiles," he
adds but tells me he finds it derogatory
to make this distinction, as though
other gentiles don't quite cut it. *In
Israel, your family would be put on
a pedestal.*
I feel a warmth.
*You should
be proud*, he says, turns and walks away.
I'm empty but for the righteousness
on my skin

Cat Got Your Tongue?

She'd come with bruises and excuses. Her name was Geesje and
she was my best friend at school. Mother dead, father and
brother to care for her and her sister. And care they did.
It was wartime, everyone taking what wasn't theirs, so
they took her, too. When Social Services got wind, they
put her in a foster home. I saw her forty years later, on
my first trip home. We cried, didn't have anything
to say, too many words, no tongue to find them.
Her name was Geesje and she
was my best
friend.

How Do You Know?

We had a woman to help with the kids.
She was Jewish, working for her keep.
My mother often talked about how their
menfolk hired themselves out;
this was how they lived.
We raised a hog in secret,
and, through the Jews we hid, sent food
to relatives who were dying of hunger
in Zuid-Holland.*
It never got there:
these poor people were running
for their lives, they were hungry, too.
I don't remember any of the Jews or
how they looked—
always wondered how you
could tell a Jew from
other people.

My Education

When I started school
there were air raids.
We were told to hide under
our desks until they were over—
my education a casualty of war.
When the potatoes were ready
each fall, I got six weeks off to help; kind
of degrading, but I kept up at
school, cried when I finished grade eight.
I wasn't allowed to go on because we
were trying
to emigrate.
It took three years.
Started working at thirteen looking after a farmer's
wife and new baby—
I learned to cook there.

Always wanted to be a nurse,
there was nursing on both sides of the family.
I would have been a good one.

21 July 2010

By nine o'clock, I'm back in the New Dorrius, having breakfast. The heavy bread, cheese, and apricots hit the spot; I'm fortified for a day of research.

I retrace yesterday's steps, walk along Staalstraat, which leads to the Waterlooplein flea market. Lingering here, I find Delft Blue trinkets for Mom and head to Rembrandt's house close by, on the Jodenbreestraat.* I love the atmosphere of this place, where many copies that his pupils have made of his work grace the walls. A demonstration of the etching process captures my attention and I watch as a young printmaker shows us how Rembrandt created some of the works for which he was best known.

After a bagel and salad at a restaurant in the city hall complex, I spend an intense afternoon in the Jewish Historical Museum (Joods Historisch Museum). Here, I learn about the Jewish population in the Netherlands during World War II, and gather context for their seeking a hiding place in my mother's village of De Krim and elsewhere. In the resource centre, librarian Anat Harel helps me with my research. I write down book titles, make photocopies, start reading an article about a Jewish refugee from Hardenberg (near De Krim), and copy the poem the Dutch Resistance used as its anthem. Anat works tirelessly to find what I need, taking a profound interest in my project. She tells me that some Dutch families made Jews pay to be harboured. Did my mother's family do this? I don't want to believe it.

Anat and I use Google Maps to trace my route to De Krim and check out the village. It's clear that Kate's plan to send me to Coevorden is the right one. We locate what I think is my mother's house—I had thought it was 137A but it's 107A, so it's quite close to the shopping plaza where the bus will drop me. De Krim seems to have blossomed—it's no longer just one street along the canal. The black-and-white photograph of my mother's house in 1943 sticks in my mind, the darkness of war all the more palpable on the water-damaged paper. I remember a starkness, as though the war had robbed all luxury—none of the affluence suggested by Google's satellite images.

When I leave Anat, I head directly to the Dutch Resistance Museum. Through interactive displays and detailed exhibits, I begin to understand the work my grandfather might have done: working on underground newspapers, altering identity cards, intercepting German communications, and sending coded messages regarding their plans to other resistance members.

I reflect that my mother's family was an honourable bunch. I had always questioned their dedication to the Dutch Reformed Church and the power it had imposed, particularly on the Dutch settlement towns in Ontario, like the one where I grew up. I remember the minister of our church ranting red-faced from the pulpit, almost chastising the congregation—often for much longer than the time allotted for the sermon. And unlike in today's churches, where Sunday school takes place during the service, the children were forced to sit through this single-minded diatribe, their Sunday school class held in the narthex after the service while their parents shared coffee, cookies, and gossip. So at tender young ages, we were subjected to the pastor's chastisement, the suggestion that we had done something wrong. I reconcile this with the fact that my mother's lot had still always tried to do what was right—maybe even because of the church's heavy hand.

On my way back to the hotel, I stop for a weiss *beer on Raadhuisstraat. I continue reading the article Anat photocopied for me, savouring the rich beer as I read about a family that took in Jews. I try to imagine how stressful it must have been for my mother's family to do so, with Nazi soldiers searching the house once, twice, three times a week.*

I gather my papers and walk back to the hotel, buy some postcards on the way, lost in thought. I feel that much closer to Mom's life, her memories.

The Librarian

In heavily accented English, she tells
me over coffee that some Dutch citizens
made Jews pay to be hidden during the war.
I don't want to believe her but I know her
shelves and cabinets of documentation must
hold some truth. She is insistent. She is Dutch
herself, speaking the wrongs of her own people.
I hold tight to my family's Christian values of
helping the hunted, take refuge in the fact that
they never exacted such payment. Months later,
I will learn that the Dutch boasted a higher rate
of turning in Jews than any other occupied
country.
Now, when I dip *speculaas** in my coffee, anticipating the
melting morsels on my tongue,
they disintegrate, crumbs sinking to
the bottom of the cup
like sediment.

The Hiding Place

It's small
I scramble in, lie down and she
covers me: layers of
cowhide, tanned and tangy.
The smell crowds my nostrils.
I will throw up.
My sweat, absorbed by the leather,
stinks more.
How many before me have lain like this?

Big boots
coming up the stairs
they walk over me
I hold my breath
I want to scream I don't dare I want out of
here what if I die and what if they forget about me

Boots on the stairs again, going down.
Door closes. I hear soft
footsteps, hear the floor slide away, feel
the leather panels lifting

The Hunting Game

He didn't brag, he didn't say anything
about it. The heroic things he did, no one
knew just what they were. He couldn't
tell us, we couldn't talk about it if he did.
We were too busy trying to be a family.
There must have been love there as my
mother was constantly pregnant. Love or
loneliness. Only years later did I grasp what
he did: blowing up bridges, destroying German
communication networks, manufacturing
identification papers for Jews, hiding them,
moving them, a kind of trafficking to safety. I
remember him telling me it was his Christian
duty to help those who were hunted. I was
too young, imagined animals and rifles, wild
game, driven by fear. I didn't understand
the chase was the same.

Negotiating with the SS

No plunging neckline, tempting
décolletage to distract.
She is well into her forties, pregnant
for the sixth time, shows in
her heavy hips and misshapen
bosom. Cannot flirt her

way out of this, nothing to
offer. Looks down, sees herself
for what she is, all womanhood,
no sexuality. Bites her
lip. This time, pure mother wit
must get her through

22 July 2010

I'm in De Krim! It's just after eleven o'clock in the morning, and I'm sitting at Café Raterink, where the bus has dropped me, having a cup of tea. My hand trembles slightly as I think about my mother. Our relationship in the last few years has been choppy, often strained. I feel I don't do enough for her—am not enough for her—and now that I have a child of my own, my thoughts are no less murky.

I understand, now, the intense love one has for a child, and the impatience at being stretched to the limit by cries and whines. And I admire how my mother managed to raise three children, virtually alone, while my father travelled incessantly. She did it with little moral support and fewer financial resources. Yet, she managed to buy us birthday and Christmas gifts and provide us with lessons when we begged—horseback riding for me, and other activities for my brother and sister. I wonder how she did it. I have one child and feel the stretch—emotional and otherwise.

I let these thoughts wash over me as I sip my warm beverage and realize that no matter what silent tirades come between us, my mother and her history have shaped me. It is her past that I look to for an understanding of my roots—of who I am, and who I can become. Her years in this tiny village are a part of me, and I understand, as I sit here, that I have come "home."

I look across the street from this outdoor patio and see a bakery and a grocery store in the town square, where I will have a lunch of bread and cheese later. It's not as small as Mom described. And the canal is beautiful, simple, peaceful. I think I saw her house as the bus drove by, but it didn't seem quite the way I remembered it from the photographs—and it wasn't number 107A, as Mom had said, but number 102. I'll soon get my bearings, and walk down the street and see.

There's a serenity here in De Krim. Certainly, the village has been modernized since Mom grew up here, but it still feels like time has stopped. The village spans a couple of kilometres along a dike, and its centre consists of a restaurant (the Café Raterink, which has a tavern, a snack bar, an ice-cream shop, and a patio) and a plaza with a grocery store, a pharmacy/hardware store rolled into one, a

bakery, and a flower shop. It's sleepy here—there's no rushing, nowhere that important to go. The stores close for lunch, reopen at one thirty. Even the bus service stops until two o'clock.

It seems that the street numbering has changed. Number 107 is a relatively new dwelling, and bears no resemblance to the house in Mom's photos. Number 102—the one I saw from the bus—looks exactly like Mom's old house, even up close. And numbers 100 and 106 don't exist, so clearly there have been some changes.

When I realize 107 doesn't make sense, I make my way to 102. The garage door is wide open, a van parked in front with its back doors spread wide, hay piled high inside. A woman, sinewy and tanned, maybe forty-five, is a few steps away. I say hello and ask if she speaks English. She smiles at me and shakes her head, and says, "My husband," and then, "he kommen,"* in her mix of Dutch and broken English. She is very kind and welcoming, and indicates that I should wait.

I comment on the rabbits and chickens I see in the nearby coop, just past a patio area with chairs and low-slung tables. I ask what other animals they have and she tells me birds, many birds.

Minutes later, I see a tall, balding man with cropped hair like my husband's walk up the path with a young, extremely pretty blond girl, who is probably about twelve or thirteen. The man, Gordon van Wezel, appears to be in his early fifties, and is handsome for his age. He has strong features, a muscular build.

I explain why I'm here—that I'm from Canada, visiting Holland for the first time, and that I believe this house was my mother's childhood dwelling. Gordon speaks easily and congenially, laughing at the coincidence that he, too, was born in Canada. Edmonton was his hometown, and he lived there from 1959, the year of his birth, until 1967, when his family went briefly to the United States before moving more permanently to Pretoria, South Africa. He is happy to speak English, and does so fluently. He is an engaging speaker and a charismatic man, and so it is a pleasant visit. He offers coffee or tea and his wife, Gaarna, goes into the house to prepare it. He gestures to the outdoor chairs and we both take a seat.

During my short stay, he tells me his life story—how he ended up in South Africa, finished his schooling, returned to the United States, and was immediately hired by the World Bank. Trained in finance, he eventually held senior positions and worked in Kenya, Nigeria, and Rotterdam, where he met and married Gaarna. Later, he bought a shipping business that sapped his energy and his family time, so his wife suggested he move on to something else. They chose De Krim for its relaxed atmosphere and change of pace. Having purchased the house nearly ten years earlier, Gordon makes excuses for the work it still requires but says that starting his business here has taken the focus away from much-needed renovations; making a living is a higher priority.

The house was built between 1929 and 1930, he says, and in the past, accommodated two families—was divided down the centre into two units. One side, the 'B' side, was a butchery. When I tell him my grandfather was a shoemaker, he says it is entirely possible that 107A had been a bootmaker's shop. (My mother later informs me that this division happened after her family sold the property, so I'm at a loss as to why it was numbered 107A when she lived there—doesn't the 'A' imply that there was also a 'B'?)

As for the number mix-up, Gordon tells me that the current 107 has been there since 1972—the previous building had been razed to make room for a more modern dwelling. He also points out that the street numbers have been revised, so maybe at some point, his house was indeed 107. At any rate, no other house on the canal strip looks like this one, so I'm quite sure this is the place. There is, too, the possibility that Mom made a mistake, though I somehow doubt she would forget her own address. It's more likely that the municipality changed the numbers (and my mother confirms it later, upon seeing my photographs). Gordon tells me that 99 and 100 were demolished, but only one building was replaced, so now there is no 100.

He tells me about De Krim. Certainly, the dialect here is very particular, with the German border being so close, and he says it is often seen as a "dumb Dutch." I explain why none of us learned to speak Dutch—that my father didn't understand my mother's dialect, and found it amusing. Gordon says he isn't surprised, and tells me that since moving here, his ten-year-old son has adopted elements of all the local dialects and is now no longer capable of speaking a proper Dutch. It worries him.

Gaarna arrives with the coffee and tea and joins us. I see a bag of tobacco and a package of cigarette papers on the table. Just like Mom and her brothers had done, these people do it the old-fashioned way and roll their own cigarettes. Not surprisingly, too, the tobacco smells strong.

Their daughter comes to sit with us, two Lhasa Apsos jumping at her heels. We embark on a very interesting discussion about family. I tell Gordon that I

36

have no sense of my father's past and don't feel the same pull to seek it out. I suggest that their attachment to their homeland is directly related to how old they were when they arrived in Canada. My mother was fifteen, my dad eleven when they set foot on Canadian shores. There's a world of difference between an eleven-year-old and a fifteen-year-old, maturity and capacity to remember the place probably playing a role here. Dad was young, ready to make a new start; Mom held on tight to the past. She remembered more and always wanted to share it; Dad wanted to assimilate.

Gordon says this makes sense to him because that's how it was back then. But he also believes that women become more attached to their surroundings. He says that for him, a move is the natural order; he has always moved and he looks at each move not as the end of something, but rather as the beginning of something else. Whereas Gaarna, he says, gets attached to wherever they live and if they were to move from De Krim, she would likely feel a sense of loss, like she was being removed from her home. I suggest that it's perhaps because women "make" the home, the nest. He agrees and smiles. A look of understanding passes between us.

He tells me that "Krimmers," as people from De Krim are called, are quite insular. They don't like accepting new people, particularly from the west of Holland. He says that when they arrived, people would make a point of not addressing them in proper Dutch, or of conversing between themselves in dialect, even if Gordon and his family were part of the conversation. He wrings his hands and says he found it rude that they wouldn't make exceptions. It was a way of shutting the new folk out, making them "other," and keeping them that way. But he accepts it—and the Krimmers have accepted him and his clan.

When I ask him if he has picked up dialect in his speech, he emphatically says, "No, and I don't want any part of it either." I realize then that Gordon, too, is hanging on to some part of his past and yet feeling like an outsider in his chosen home. This is exactly what Nancy Huston was talking about in Losing North. Gordon has lost north, too.

By this point, Gaarna and their young daughter have left us. Gordon finishes his cigarette, tells me he must soon be in De Krim for a meeting, and offers to show me the house. Once inside, I see Gaarna is busy tidying. He laughs and says, "She's asking me, 'Why today of all days, to show someone, when things are such a mess?'" I try to make her understand how grateful I am for their hospitality. The kitchen is small, clean, and organized, with armoires in light wood

A view of the house that shows the sheer silk damask drapes and hints of the antique-doll collection on the windowsills.

and shiny stainless-steel appliances. A pink salmon colour on the walls gives it warmth.

Gordon leads me to the living room, which has a partial wall down the centre. He explains that this is how it must have been divided for the two families who once lived here. Now, one side houses a family room/play area for the kids with a television and games console. The other side has a wood stove and hearth with a massive, streamlined maple hutch. Two soft leather sofas are placed nearby to create an intimate square. On the large windowsill are antique dolls in flowing nineteenth-century-style gowns. The windows are dressed in a sheer, burgundy, iridescent damask, hanging in bunches over a rod, the light catching its golden folds. I imagine my mother sitting on that sill, hear the hiss of aircraft and the sounds of bombs exploding in the distance. I know these luxurious draperies were not part of the scene.

Before leaving, I take a photo of Gordon and his family so that I can show my mother who lives here now. Despite protests from his wife, they all comply. Gordon explains to his son and daughter what I want and why I'm here, laughter *in his voice, and they gather in an affectionate stance and smile. Afterwards, I shake Gordon's hand, say thank you and goodbye.*

I return to the village square, stopping first at the grocery store to purchase Gouda cheese, a hunk of rye bread, bottled water, and a package of gevulde kanos, *my favourite almond finger cookies, fondly remembered from childhood. I sit on a bench and quietly tear the bread, adorning each piece with savoury slices of cheese. It's hard to imagine my mother running in that backyard from air raids, but a property holds many secrets. I know it happened and now I've seen the place. Somehow that's enough.*

Motherlode
Hoofdweg* 102, De Krim, Overijssel

Flatlands, farm
country, waterways,
treelines.
Train speeding me back
in time to this quiet village,
barely awake. I walk along the
dike, thinking of the boy
who stuck his finger in, legend
like my mother's house—until today.

Its façade, triangular with two windows
upstairs, two larger ones at
ground level, looks like a
face with wide eyes and a
large mouth, expressions and
words, stories to tell.

Once a butchery and a
shoemaking shop, now
home to a family of
six. Front room
divided by need—
PlayStation and TV on
one side, hearth and soft
leather sofas on the other

no trace of her life,
no visible false ceiling,
no frame around
untold stories.

My Mother's Voice

Right behind the house was Papa's aviary—did you know that if you feed carrots to canaries, they turn orange?—and behind that, an overhang with beehives underneath. Mama would sell the honey in the store—sweet, good honey. Two sour-cherry trees against the beehive building, we'd get up there to pick cherries. Before Papa built the aviary, there was a sweet-cherry tree and Mama used to do them up in jars—everything was done up in jars in those days because there were no freezers—you know, like chutney and jam. We had a large cellar with many shelves where everything was stored in winter. That's where we went when the air raids were on. Behind the aviary, we grew potatoes, beans, carrots, onions, and peas—it sounds like we had enough, doesn't it?—but the soldiers asked for a lot and we had to give it to them. My garden was at the very end of our land; I grew asters, marigolds, dahlias, and daisies. Deep ditches separated our property from the neighbour's. Sometimes people hid in them and got shot by the Germans. After the war, we played hide-and-seek in those ditches, completely forgot the bodies that fell there.

The Root Cellar

We shimmy down the stairs,
lights out, damp
and dirt beneath our feet
the din of sirens
then
kaboom.
The walls shake.
Grit in mouths and
stinging eyes, our hands trace the
wall for balance.
We slip on the worn stone steps
our ears
ring.
Trembling in fear, we fumble
for the cellar latch,
creak.
We step in, breathing sharply,
and close the door,
click.
Sitting now on the dirt floor,
we see the jars of cherry preserves
glinting in the darkness,
and
look down at our protruding
empty bellies, lick our
lips and remember the taste
as the house
shudders
once again.

The Hunger Winter, 1944–45

I remember
my small hands pulling up his covers,
being startled by his raspy breath
coming from a mouth, a face, I didn't recognize—
my father was oh so thin.
I must have been six when I saw him
there on the divan in the living room
bright light filtering in,
scattering on a hollow face.

I remember
Mama offering thin soups made of vegetables from jars in the cellar,
from potatoes she had hidden under straw.
We had just enough
but he and his fellow resistance fighters
ate tulip bulbs, toxins from their onion-like centres
coursing through bodies covered
in skin and bone—bodies fighting
two wars.

After that
tulips never looked the same to me.

1942: My mother at the age of four. Despite hardship, her smile was genuine.

A Conversation
May 2013

Her voice sounds far away, like she's trying desperately to grasp something that keeps slipping away. It's been a while since we talked about this, and it's as though she has built up a resistance to going back to that place in her childhood. "I'd really have to work to get there," she says quietly, "and I don't know if I want to." Nevertheless, I hear her becoming small, with large eyes, watching her sick father on a cot in the living room. "I can picture him," she says. "He was so thin. There was no nutrition in those tulip bulbs, and he was weak to start with." He'd come home from working for the Resistance in Lisse, a part of the Netherlands that had not yet been liberated. How he'd even gotten home is outside of her recollection. "He'd also contracted tuberculosis, which complicated things," she adds.

Her thoughts wander, as though I'm not there. She's talking to herself—or to the six-year-old girl she once was. "We had enough to eat—we had a garden that gave us just what we needed. I didn't have to eat tulip bulbs. Even though we were close to the German border, they didn't bomb our gardens, which were long strips at the end of the property." I've seen her house and the long narrow grounds, so I can easily picture what she's telling me. "Mom canned everything— carrots, potatoes. And the carrots were rooted in the dirt floor of the cellar." Her voice is more confident, the images becoming firmer as she recalls. "The potatoes were outside, buried under soil, then covered in straw. The radio was there, too."

I've heard most of this before, but I never tire of hearing it again. I let her talk, not daring to interrupt the stream of consciousness that is her memory. Then there's something new, a tiny window into that time: "I remember helping with the dishes. I would stand on a stool and wash them in a pan of soapy water and Mom would dry." Her voice cracks. I see her there, with bright red locks and front teeth missing, and I feel a tug at my insides. Reconcile this with an image of my own son at a similar age and realize that motherhood equalizes everything between us. Her and her own mother. Her and me. Me and my son. These things transcend time and experience, and in that moment, we blur into one.

The Walls Have Ears

Nobody thinks I know, but I do. I've seen and heard it all, words bouncing off these walls, leaving traces. Bits of conversation, faint echoes clinging like paint to the frame. SS officers search the house with stern expressions, their stiff black uniforms and starched ties reflecting the tension of each moment. Hennie leading them through each room with deliberate, rehearsed composure. But I've seen her tremble and sob upon their leaving. She is tough, but hardly immune to the noxious residue of their power. Here in the attic room where Wim stored the shop leather goods, my walls smell of rawhide and fear. I can still see the Jewish families huddle and scrunch into tight balls, as though that tightness will make them disappear. I wonder how, in that tiny space, they manage to bear it without passing out, the stench of nervous sweat and bodily odours mixed with the tang of musty leather. They're alone and lonely and don't know what each day holds. And every time there's a knock at the door, I can sense their mouths go dry, their stomachs constrict. They believe they are already dead. How many times can you feel death so close without little parts of you dying, particle by particle? Alive in a dying husk of a body, rattled by the options, each one no less terrifying than the next. I'm glad to be a house, just a mess of boards and stone clapped together, easily toppled, easily forgotten. Yet, living, I absorb each sentiment, every mood—desire, hatred, loathing, sadness, fear, pain. All caught in my plaster like a fungus, leeching my walls, buried but still alive there.

Where We Hid Them

I was two years old when
the war started. It was all I knew.
What was my mother like? She
did what was asked of her. We were
occupied, so she had no choice but
to do as she was told. The German soldiers
were okay, sometimes they didn't want
to do things but had no choice. It was the
SS—they were the nasty ones. We didn't
understand German but
here and there
words were the same, you got
the gist of it.
They searched the house,
always at night.
They didn't know we had a double
floor between the first and second
storeys where we hid people. We
were lucky they never
found it. We'd have been
deported to a work camp
or shot.

22 July 2010

This evening, it looks like it will soon erupt into a downpour, so I duck into a shop on the Haarlemmerstraat, Het Grote Avontuur—the Big Adventure. I had visited on my first day here in a haze of jet lag, and was taken with the milk-painted rustic cabinets and unusual trinkets, to the point that I even took photos. Now, I select small gifts for friends and family.

As I pay, I strike up a conversation with the shopkeeper. I tell her that my mother would love this store, that she collects Delft Blue and would adore some of the dishes on display. Without condescension, she tells me that the dishes are not from Delft but from France—that I must have assumed they were Dutch because of their tulip pattern. I explain that my mother is Dutch and that while I know that Delft Blue is probably a bit clichéd here in Holland, she still likes it, no doubt because it reminds her of home. The shop owner, whose name I later learn is Anna Massee, asks me where she is from, and so I tell her about my visit to De Krim today. She has no idea where De Krim is, though she knows of the neighbouring town, Coevorden.

I tell her of my experience there, and we start talking about Dutch people speaking English so well. I recount my visit to the Jewish Historical Museum, where the librarian had explained that so many Dutch learn their English from television because it isn't dubbed like it is in Germany. Dutch people hear the dialogue as they read the subtitles and therefore absorb English from an early age, in addition to learning it in school.

Anna is curious, and asks me what's driving my research. I explain that I'm a writer trying to piece together my mother's wartime childhood. "I went to the Jewish Historical Museum to learn about the Dutch hiding Jews during World War II—because my mother's family did that and I want to understand not just the Jewish perspective, but especially the Dutch experience, of people risking their lives to do what they thought was right."

I explain that the museum librarian was able to provide much information and that I had photocopied, read, and already learned a great deal. "But do you know what she told me?" I ask her. "She told me that many Dutch people made Jews pay to be hidden."

"Oh, no, I don't think it's as many as she suggests," Anna responds. Her tone is firm.

"I hope you're right," I offer. "I know that my grandparents did not make them pay." I say this with conviction but the truth is, I have no idea. (It will be one of the first things my mother will confirm for me upon my return to Canada. "As Christians," she will say, "it was our duty to help those who were being hunted. There is no doubt my family would have been deported to a concentration camp if it had ever been discovered.")

Anna continues. "Like I said, I don't think it's that many. And if they did, maybe it was because it was the only source of income they had." She understands my need for this not to be true. "Of course, in war, there are always people who exploit others, but I believe that if they could help, they did," she adds.

"Certainly, here in Amsterdam, there are many stories of the Dutch helping the Jews—and I have never heard of them exacting payment," she says. I'm sure that the librarian's information is factual—that it's based on research and documentation. But Anna's reaction makes me want to believe that it was not a rampant practice.

I like her forthrightness—and I like her. Dark-haired, blue-eyed, and voluptuous, she is not of the same strain of Dutch as I am—no lanky body and blond hair to be found here. She proceeds to tell me a story of her own, equally arresting.

"My grandfather worked for the Dutch Resistance, too," she begins. "When my grandmother was pregnant with my mother, he died doing underground work." She goes on to explain that her grandfather was killed in May, leaving her grandmother a young widow with an unborn child. "He was a young man whose job was to plant bombs along the railway lines to thwart the Germans' use of them," she explains. There were many accidents with these rudimentary bombs, she says, and her grandfather was the victim of one such accident.

"My grandmother also did underground work," Anna adds quietly. "Fully pregnant, she would carry her secret basket. No one knew what she was carrying—I'm not even sure she knew—but she brought things in her basket to help the cause."

I'm riveted. I realize as we talk that the stories I could uncover are many. I tell her that my recent visit to the Dutch Resistance Museum helped me gain a deeper understanding of underground work, and what tasks my grandfather might have taken on. I point out that my mother has no idea, even to this day—and she doesn't believe my grandmother even knew.

Anna asks me how long I'm staying and I explain that my five-day foray is ending in two short days. "But it sounds like you have made the most of it— you've gotten what you came for," she says warmly. Yes, she's right. I have. "You must make something of this," she adds quietly. "It's an incredible story." She asks me to let her know if I publish something, and inscribes her email address on her store brochure.

A little later, as I sit in the San Pedro Argentinian restaurant a few doors down from Anna's store, the rain pummelling violently outside, I realize the evening's outing adds to a framework of stories, poems, and other writings that has already begun to form.

Stimpie Stampie* at the New Dorrius

This, in what's billed as
Fresh Dutch Cuisine, is more refined—
potatoes, kale, back bacon, pearl onions
with rich gravy, meatballs served with
spicy Dutch mustard from Zaandam
goes up my nose,
tells me it's real—
here and now
not quite the *boerenkool* my mother
used to make. We called it
farmer's cabbage—peasant's dish—
kale cooked soft, mixed with mashed
potatoes and sausages, swimming in a
velvet gravy that slid over the tongue.
I know now she was recreating home
when she made it, fuelled by
nostalgia, dislocation—
trying to give us what
she was missing

The Bartender

No wine tonight? asks Javed
Ahktar, who's been serving here
for thirty-two years. *No*, I say, *a quiet tea
is all I need. You are still writing?* he
asks, trying not to pry. *Yes,* I say and
tell him of my journey. Asks if I
am a journalist, why my mother
didn't come along. He knows
aging parents, understands that
they don't always get it, plans
to visit his own mother in Pakistan
in September. He goes home to find
his, I leave home to find
　　　mine.

The Red Boots

She has been waiting
for days to show me
the red boots, pulls me
into the store
Smell the leather, my daughter
cries, running her hands
along the fine workmanship
I take the boot
bring it to my nose, feel
the swell of memory, searing,
burning my nostrils. I am
back in Father's shoemaking
shop in our small Dutch
village, the tanned hides
stacked one upon
the other
disguising the hollow in
the floor where we hid
Jews, smell of life, smell
of death, those who escaped,
those who died trying, all the
faces I can't remember. Buy them,
I say. They make such a statement.
But she can't possibly know
just what I mean

Listening to the Radio

We had a radio, too,
hidden in the potatoes in
the garden behind the house.
God knows what would have
happened to us if they'd
found it, with Dad working
underground and all.
A teacher at our school,
Meester van der Kolk,
got arrested near the
end of the war
for listening,
was released when
the Canadians
freed Holland.

The SS Came at Night

Sometimes two or three times
a week
to check the house,
looking for my dad,
who they suspected worked
underground.
My mom was afraid
with all these little kids around.
Dad did come home
sometimes
because two of my brothers
were born during the war.

23 July 2010

I start the day with a walk to the Rijksmuseum, which is under major renovation. Only twelve rooms displaying the Old Masters are open. One of them houses Rembrandt's The Night Watch. *I stand in front of it for almost an hour, overwhelmed by its severity, its darkness, and the strange play of light on the canvas. It's huge—and at that, was cut down on all four sides in 1715, the reduction of the left side resulting in two people being cut out. The painting has quite a history: In 1975, unemployed schoolteacher Wilhelmus de Rijk attacked the work with a bread knife, leaving large zigzag slashes. Though the work was restored, there is still evidence of the damage. The culprit committed suicide in 1976. Then, in 1990, a man sprayed acid on the canvas with a concealed pump bottle. Security guards intervened just in time and the acid penetrated only the varnish. The painting was again restored.*

It fascinates me that this work could inspire such acts of violence. I stand there, suddenly struck by all the violence this trip has forced me to contemplate—the violence of the war and its residual effects on my mother, and on so many others.

Following my visit, I have lunch at a small café on the Spiegelgracht,* very close to the museum. I pick at the innards of my sandwich as I watch people walk by.

I make several stops for souvenirs on the way back to the hotel, and, along the Herengracht,* stop at the Netherlands Institute for War Documentation, a library that houses the world's largest collection of World War II materials. In addition, it is the Center for Holocaust and Genocide Studies. Upon entering, I consult the librarian, who shows me how to access the institute's online catalogue (they use a system I am not familiar with, neither Library of Congress nor Dewey).

I sit at a computer terminal and end up finding a number of interesting sources, many of which have been published in North America and can be procured from home. Surprisingly, two of my most interesting finds are published by the small Ontario publishers Seraphim Editions and Second Story Press, probably because of the great numbers of Dutch immigrants who came to small Ontario towns. Much of what I find is written from the Jewish perspective.

I come across writings by Louis de Jong, a Dutch historian who was director of the institute for many years. This man spoke at conferences and wrote many articles—most, if not all of which are collected here.

I find specific writings on helping Jews written from the Dutch non-Jewish perspective, as well as other material on life for Jews and non-Jews in Nazi-occupied Holland. One book, Quiet Heroes: True Stories of the Rescue of Jews by Christians in Nazi-occupied Holland, *by André Stein, published in 1988, is a collection of several stories based on interviews that Stein conducted. Reading this, I feel the wind knocked out of me. Here are stories I am certain strongly resemble the stories my mother has told me—with the Christian aspect well-documented. (When I return to Canada, I will manage to get a used copy of* Quiet Heroes *on Amazon and will be jolted all over again by the inscription to the previous owner on the inside cover: "To remember your grandfather and granduncles from 1940–1945 and all the uncles and second cousins who gave their lives so others would live. From your mother with much love.")*

After I leave the institute, I stop at a bakery to buy freshly baked speculaas, *my favourite Dutch spice biscuits. They're still hot—and are by far the best I've ever eaten. I get that odd feeling again—of being home, of feeling like I belong.*

Later in the day, I decide to visit the Museum Amstelkring, now called Ons' Lieve Heer op Solder (Museum Our Lord in the Attic). A number of stoned young men stumble out of coffee houses into my path as I trace and retrace my steps, trying to find my way. It's the first time during my stay that I long for home.

I finally find the museum on the Oudezijds Voorburgwal.* Inside, I'm reminded that there was once a ban on Catholicism in this now-liberal city. During the Reformation, when Catholics were forbidden to hold public services, they built this clandestine sanctuary across three attics. It makes me think of the attic sanctuary in my mother's childhood home, where her family hid fleeing Jews.

Later, I enjoy an hour-long canal cruise, which takes me into the main harbour and all the places I've already visited on foot. I realize it's my last view of this city, which has worked its way into my heart and mind.

Speculaas on the Prinsengracht

Used to the store-bought biscuits that make
their cross-ocean journey, the kind my
big-boned Dutch relatives dipped into
steaming coffee.
I am intoxicated by the
ruddy mix of allspice and cloves, the crumbling
texture of brown sugar, heat
on my fingers from an oven housed in
terracotta brick, I shimmy along the
Prinsengracht, feeling a part of the landscape
that evades me at home.
Scent of ginger on my
hands, I try to harness the smell, the
taste of memory but
I know
it too will elude me
upon my leaving

Alarm

"Let's run over it again, shall we?" The local volunteer fire chief, Jack Kemp, says this to Trijntje Meijer as she pulls up a chair. He is already seated at the table in her large but cluttered kitchen, pouring copious amounts of cream into the mug of coffee she has just served. Ginger cookies that the Dutch settlers call *speculaas* are stacked on the plate in front of him. He knows he should resist but takes one anyway, ever aware of his growing waistline.

"Yes, just to be sure," Trijntje responds to his suggestion. "I wouldn't want to get it wrong."

She is a bustling woman in her late fifties, always wearing an apron. Her Dutch accent is still pronounced after more than thirty-five years in Canada. She still hasn't mastered the word "three," which always comes out as a rasping "sree," making her grown children giggle when they hear it.

Jack Kemp is here because Trijntje and her husband, Broos, have recently bought the village store and gas bar, and part of their new community role is to call the force of volunteer firefighters to duty. The station is adjacent to the store, which is attached to their country home.

"You'll get a call on that phone," Jack Kemp says, pointing to the old rotary-dial red phone on the wall near the door that connects her kitchen and the store. He has already told her that she is not to answer the call—the ring itself, which is particularly shrill, is her cue. "As soon as you hear it, grab the keys and get over to the station. Unlock the man-door, yank the siren switch, and then go into the garage and unlock the big doors from the inside. The siren will alert the men and when they get here, they'll just have to pull up the doors to get to the trucks. It's pretty straightforward, Mrs. Meijer."

"It sounds easy enough," Trijntje answers. "I just hope that the phone doesn't stress me out so much that I forget something important." Her demeanour is completely calm—no one would ever guess that Trijntje had once been a bundle of nerves. Growing up in Nazi-occupied Holland, building a life in a new land, raising her five children, and managing her once-wandering husband have strengthened her, made her capable of handling just about anything. It's true, too, that she is calmer since coming to Canada—a country where nothing ever happens and people are always safe. And though she'll never quite forget the sounds of war, they're far enough away now that she can relax. It's 1986 after all—the war has been over for more than forty years.

"Just leave the key hanging by the phone," Kemp suggests, dipping his *speculaas* into his coffee just like he has seen his Dutch friends do. In this part of rural Ontario, where Dutch settlement communities abound, it is not an uncommon sight. The cookie melts in his mouth, offering a feeling of comfort that suits Mrs. Meijer's Delft-blue kitchen. "That way, you'll never have to ask yourself where you put them."

"That's a good idea," she says, nodding her head as her hands fold around her warm mug of coffee. "I hadn't thought about moving it, but now that you mention it, I'll make sure that Broos wasn't thinking we should hang it with our own keys here in the kitchen."

"All right, Mrs. Meijer, I guess I should be on my way. Thank you for the coffee and cookies." Kemp smiles warmly at this woman, who seems completely confident in her brisk, energetic way.

After he leaves, Trijntje quietly puts the coffee cups and the mostly eaten plate of cookies on the counter, and wanders back into the store. As she tidies up, serves gas, and helps customers, she thinks about Chief Kemp's visit. *I'm too old for this*, she says to herself. But she also knows that if that phone does ring, she'll be fine.

❧

It's a rainy, mild autumn night as Trijntje begins her routine closing of the store. Broos has gone to help a local farmer organize a load of hay bales. She misses him when he's not there and smiles as she thinks of his wiry old body, once taut and straight—he was once handsome enough to turn all the heads in town. Though the early part of their almost thirty-year marriage wasn't easy, she thinks of him with only fondness now. She hardly blames all those women for looking—nor does she any longer blame him for having been tempted. It's water under the bridge, she thinks, sighing, and they are bound by years of happy companionship. She hopes he's not getting too wet working with those soggy rolls of hay.

She looks at her checklist for stocking and closing up: Enough ice in the cooler? *Ja.* * Covers on the gas pumps? *Ja.* Drinks fridge stocked? *Ja.* Candy and gum racks full? *Ja.* Enough cigarette packages? *Ja.* Lottery tickets neatly placed under the plastic cover? *Ja.* Door locked? "*Ja,*" she says aloud, as she presses her fingers to her forehead, suddenly completely spent. Feeling lonely and exhausted, Trijntje looks at the cigarettes, neatly arranged in rows on the shelf behind the cash. *If I smoked, now would be a good time,* she muses. She walks up the steps and into the house, pulling the flimsy door closed behind her.

Her thoughts turn to the evening meal and she feels bleak at the prospect of eating without Broos. As she opens the refrigerator door, she considers her options. Broos's special homemade macaroni and cheese or her favourite Dutch dish, *boerenkool,* a mixture of boiled kale and mashed potatoes with sausages—an old-country casserole that she still loves, despite the fact that it was one of the few items on the menu during the war. It's still comfort food. *Ja, boerenkool,* she thinks. *That will make me feel better.* She pulls the pot out, and as she turns to set it on the counter, the phone rings. Trijntje puts the pot down quickly and wipes her hands on her apron, looks for the handset. When she finds it under Broos's newspaper on the kitchen table, she holds it with a puzzled look. *It's not ringing.* With a sharp intake of breath, she looks towards the red wall phone.

Despite the tight panic in Trijntje's limbs, Chief Kemp's words come back to her: *"As soon as you hear it, grab the key and get over to the station. Unlock the man-door, yank the siren switch, and then go into the garage and unlock the big doors from the inside."*

Miraculously—almost mechanically—Trijntje pulls herself together, briefly muttering, "Oh, Broos, where are you?" as her ample form charges towards the key hanging by the phone. She flips it into her apron pocket, turns with surprising speed, shoves her feet into gardening clogs, unlocks the patio door, and steps into the damp evening air. She moves fast through the wet grass, her buxom silhouette almost gliding over the grounds towards the fire station. Fingers wound tightly around the key ring, she draws it from her apron pocket and primes the key for entry into the lock, turns it efficiently, and pushes the door open.

Her eyes quickly scan the station, barely seeing the fire trucks to her left or the kitchen area with a table and chairs before she zeroes in on the red lever with "SIREN" written above it. Dropping the key back into her pocket without thinking, she rushes to the lever and pulls it down. Hearing the siren's wails, Trijntje stands stock-still, then sinks to her knees and huddles in a ball, a terrified scream coming from the very depths of her lungs. She automatically looks skywards, searching for the bombers, even as she hears her father yelling to keep her head down, her eyes closed. But she has to know where the planes are. She has to know if death is about to drop itself on her in a raging ball of fire. Her teenage mind wants to be prepared. The air-raid siren is deafening, ringing in her ears beyond the sounds of her shrieking siblings and neighbours, beyond the ground-shaking explosions. Trijntje does not see the station's ceiling, but a darkened sky with flashes of light as bombs explode on the horizon. As the siren reaches its full pitch, then falls into the lower notes, Trijntje's scream somehow continues, though she no longer sees anything, just fire, the acrid burning of wood filling her nostrils, the smell of fear overwhelming her senses.

Suddenly, strong arms envelop her. The siren has stopped but she is still wailing uncontrollably. "Papa, Papa," she sobs. "*Zijn ze weg? Zijn we veilig?*" *Are they gone? Are we safe?*

Jack Kemp holds Trijntje tight to him, strokes her grey hair, tells her, "Yes, Mrs. Meijer, they're gone. Don't worry, we're safe." Trijntje grabs his shoulders, presses her frame against him, hides her face in a body she is convinced is her father's, and weeps.

Kemp looks up as his men don flame-proof coats and gloves, preparing for the real fire. He asks his second-in-command to get a hold of Trijntje's husband and says he'll be along shortly. "Throw me a blanket before you go," he adds.

Kemp unfolds the thermal cover, pulls it around Trijntje's shoulders. The bustling, robust woman he shared coffee and cookies with a fortnight ago is a gaunt shadow, an old woman in a tired apron with a hollowness in her eyes. She is dazed, still not quite aware of her surroundings. Kemp feels a sudden exhaustion, a deep sadness. Her mutterings in Dutch and her rolled-into-a-ball contortions had given him quick insight—how could he have known that the station's siren would send her back to war-torn Holland? He shakes his head at his own stupidity. He wishes he had told her what to expect. He should have played her a demo tape or something. His arms around her, he feels her give way to sleep, her body finally surrendering. He eases her from under his arm, lays her head gently on his jacket, and waits for her husband to arrive.

24 July 2010

It's five o'clock in the morning, and I'm on the train to Schiphol* in a car full of noisy Brits. The day has begun awry. My hotel bill was incorrect and sorting it with the desk staff made my timing tight. Then, when I arrived at the train station, the train attendant told me my ticket was stamped on the wrong end, and that I needed to go do it again. An American trio had walked up to the platform with me and hadn't stamped theirs at all. I pointed this out to the attendant. He didn't care, sent me back. I left my luggage with the Americans and sprinted back to the stamping machine, all the while wondering whether I should trust anyone with my bags.

I take a deep breath. Everything is fine now. I'm on the way to Schiphol, on my way home.

The real work lies ahead: drawing this material together to write the book that is now running rampant in my mind. I have a more complete picture, now, of my mother as a small child—and of the insurmountable difficulties her own mother faced trying to keep her many children safe and fill their hungry bellies while hiding Jews under floorboards. I'm starting to hear their voices in my head, all fighting to be heard. Finding a way for them to speak aloud is the task now. I'm ready for it.

Chapter Two

The Children

The War Begins

My father in the living room
listening to the BBC
hears the Germans have invaded Poland
I waltz in wearing my *dirndl*, traditional
German dress with tight bodice and frills, so
popular in Holland. He takes one look,
yells at me, "Get that thing off!"
He'd bought a boat, docked it in Amsterdam,
expected to leave in it if the Germans invaded;
they bombed the harbour, the boat with it
No more dirndls, no more escape plan

Onderduik, 1944

Try to imagine the small
body, pudgy face, carrot
hair. Resistance fighter
at six. Papa underground, the work
never stops.
Brows pinched, she
reads the signs, must get a
message out. They know what we
are doing,
they know, they know, they know.
Bundles the flowers in a basket,
gets Mama to write a note in code.
Move the family NOW, it says.
Carries the message buried
in silky petals, stalks of green.
Here, she says, take it. Goes to
school, pretends all is normal.

We All Took Part

Even my brother
who was only six.
One day, he came tearing
down the street,
underground newspapers
hidden in his boots—
gleefully proclaiming that
no one knew.
He called the soldiers *moffen* *
in unrestrained tones,
scared the bejesus out of me.
If he'd been caught,
they'd have shot
him
on the spot.

The Risks He Took

He was courageous, that boyfriend.
Marinus was his name. I was sixteen, sick with
double pneumonia, always ill. Lack of food
in wartime, I could never get better. He dared
ask the farmers for food, did it for me,
risked his life to get milk. Barely a man,
would have been executed
if they'd told on him.

Learning Curve

It was my first year
of high school
a Christian *lycée*
(I was far from being Christian).
In no time
the Germans
commissioned the building
kicked us out.
We were put
in two different villas
in Haarlem.
There was no school
during the last two years
of the war,
no teachers,
no heat,
no food.
I learned what it was like
to do without.

Soldier Boy

Where are you, the young
boy I often dreamed of?
Tall, blond, sharp
features made all the
more pointed by your
perfectly pressed uniform.
All these years later, I
still think of you, standing guard
in our village, looking so stern,
then occasionally winking at me
quickly, shyly, mischievously.
Your smile was a rain shower
in affection's drought.
But you were a German soldier
and I could never know you.

Christmas Eve 1943

What a disgrace—
my uncle,
an NSB'er
managing a farm
for the Germans
on the border between
Holland and Belgium.
My brother and I visited,
Christmas 1943.
Air raid on the train,
strafing—
planes trying to blow up the engines.
We were all told
to get off,
lay in ditches
cold and wet.
Don't remember how we got
to my uncle's.
Midnight Mass on Christmas Eve,
half in Belgium, half in
Holland.
I remember the clear night air
walking to the church
in fresh fallen snow.

The Beef Tongue

I learned to smuggle
early in life.
I was nine,
with mother
bringing home meat
from a farm.
She carried most of it
in her bag,
gave me the beef tongue,
tied around my waist,
hid in layers of
a long skirt—my grandmother's.
Miserable tongue hanging
between my legs.
Don't know how they
wrapped it so it wouldn't
bleed all over.
A bouquet of flowers to
cover it,
imagining girls in the train
laughing at my
hanging tongue.

Wool Was Hard to Get

There was no room to store the sweaters
and socks we'd grown out of
Mama unravelled them all, made new
from old
Comforting sound of her needles clicking,
knowledge that we might be warmer
come morning

The Collection

We imagined the explosions, how they
deformed the metal, made them into works of art.
We had a contest to see
who could collect the most unusual pieces:
shape, length, sharpness.

This was war, benign behind the front lines
until the day the Allied forces launched an air attack
on our town. Column of German soldiers
walking our street, noise of car and truck engines drowning
out the roar of air-raid sirens, grandfather screaming at us
to get inside, seek cover in the sub-basement. When it was over,
he let us come up but wouldn't let us outside, bits of
bodies littered the street. Afterwards, we threw out our pieces,
never looked for shrapnel again.

The Walnut Tree

We wanted
those walnuts, rare treats,
growing on a tree behind the house commissioned
by the Germans.
On the way home from school
we'd sneak
into the garden, pick nuts from the tree, crack
their shells, hurriedly dig out the meat.
One day, we froze as we
noticed a German officer looking
down on us.
We waited
for his anger.
Instead, in low tones, he
told us to come back any time.
We thought
how nice these German soldiers are.
Two days later, they rounded up
Dutch saboteurs
and shot them in the street.

The American Soldier

She told me not to go without my brother
but I didn't listen.
Young men in uniform were everywhere in this house,
our two rooms cramped.
Not much to do and Mama always needed
more space, quiet for the baby.
I looked in the mirror
before leaving, twisted the
deep purple scarf around my neck
one more time, tossed my head.
Carefree sophisticate.
He invited me up to the roof.
He made me feel interesting
and not eleven.
We took the steps
two at a time, hand in hand,
a game that ended
at the top.
Looked across the fields, scarf blowing
in the stiff breeze—
Then his hands were on my pancake breasts and
the hard thing between his legs pushing
on my crotch.
He coaxed, voice with rough edges. I brought my
knee up, heard him gasp as he faltered.
I flew down the stairs, felt the scarf
sail away in the wind.

What Lisbeth Knows

Lisbeth so young but
she knows
something so wrong.
She is staying at Tante Jannie's
(relief from chaos in Nijmegen)
but Jews still fearful here in Oss.
Lisbeth knows
the family across the street is Jewish,
sees the small baby in his papa's arms
Next day, same baby with another man
acting like a papa, too
Lisbeth
nudges her mama.
Why? she asks. *Why?*
You did not see that child,
she answers.
You did not see.
Lisbeth so young but
she knows
to be quiet.

No Visible Injury

They kept telling her to
be quiet
SSSShhhhhh
They'd put a finger to their lips—
Don't talk about this
You didn't see that
She went through her childhood
in a whisper
or with no voice at all
saw no *onderduikers**
saw no Jews
told no lies
hid nothing
stole nothing
was nothing

God in de Hemel*

Sirens blaring through the night
In this chaos a new life
Papa goes to church
to pray for the baby Petra
until Mama gives birth

Next day, we eat biscuits with pink
and white sprinkles to celebrate
and Papa baptizes Petra, afraid
she won't go to heaven if
we die

He calls the priest again
in the morning in case he got
it wrong. Petra was baptized
twice but it never made her
into a believer

Bittersweet

More than a year of occupation
and fruit rarely to be
found.
Our generous German keepers
bring oranges from Spain into
the schools, make us eat them
at our desks. Mother has me smuggle home
the peels
for flavouring

The Bouquet

Brigitta had dug the soil herself, creating small plots with pathways in between. The asters and dahlias she had planted last fall were now flowering and she walked the footpaths to tend them, using small hands to pull a dead stalk or pop off a wilted flower. Her father had managed to find two kinds of dahlias—a friend had given him bulbs for lemon elegance, an angry-looking yellow flower with bunched stringy petals, and now it was in full bloom. Brigitta felt like they were yelling at her, these spiky blossoms, and she couldn't hold back a smile.

The other dahlia was the clair de lune, also yellow but with eight harmonious heart-shaped petals around an orange centre. Somehow they added balance to the screaming lemon strain. She had planted these around the edges of the small plot so they surrounded the lemon elegance. It was as though they kept the others in check, whipping their angry neighbours into order.

She moved to the next plot, her six-year-old eyes sizing up the gladioluses, tulips, and asters. Her father would always tell her that she was the youngest professional gardener he knew. He would pinch her cheeks when he said it. "You're better than me," he would say. "Your thumb isn't just green, it's the colour of every flower in your garden." She would swell with pride. There wasn't much to be good at in a war, but she had found her thing.

"Brigitta!" Her older brother's voice interrupted the few happy thoughts she managed these days. "They're going to tell on us! *We've got to do something!*" Johannes was gasping for air as he ran towards her. "We have to tell Mama and she has to tell Papa. She has to get a message to him."

"What do you mean?" Brigitta tried to keep her voice steady. "Who is going to tell? And what do they know, anyway?"

"I talked to Willem in the village. He said the Schaaps are going to tell the Germans that Papa is coming home. Willem said that if they tell the SS, they'll be protected." Johannes was still breathing hard.

Brigitta felt old and exhausted. Although he was four years older, Johannes always came to her when he was worried.

She dropped the stalks she had pruned and gathered herself. "Let's go tell Mama. She'll know what to do." Brigitta knew the first order of business was telling an adult. Odo, one of her father's resistance colleagues, lived on the other side of the canal. He had a bad leg and had not been conscripted for German factory work. He was always at home, looking after his family—and plenty of resistance activities, too. Brigitta was already thinking that Mama would tell her to take a message to Odo that Papa was on the SS list and should not come home this weekend. They'll shoot him if they find him, she thought. That's what happened to their neighbour not too long ago. He came up from underground when the SS happened to be looking for him. When he was climbing the fence between their properties to come visit Papa, they shot him. Just like that. She remembered his limp form hanging from the fence post. The adults had to go down after dark and remove him, and bring his body to his wife.

She stopped suddenly. A message would be better hidden in something. "Wait," she said to her brother. Quickly, she picked up the clippers and lopped off a rough bouquet of tulips, gladioluses, zinnias, asters, and pink roses. She didn't touch the lemon elegance or the clair de lune. "Let's go," she said. With the flowers under one arm, she and Johannes strode up the walk towards the house.

Toos's gaze moved from the soup pot to her children's anxious faces and she set down the ladle. "What is it?" she asked, quickly acknowledging the panic in their expressions. As usual, Johannes was speechless. She wondered, not for the first time, why her oldest boy could not force the words out under duress. Also not for the first time, she blamed the war: fear had silenced his normally quick tongue.

"Mama!" said Brigitta, and Toos knew that her small daughter was once again taking control in a manner that was well beyond her years. In a few short sentences, she repeated what Johannes had told her. Before her mother could find a solution, Brigitta suggested coding a message and bringing it to Odo's house in the flowers. "We can roll it up and slide it into the stalk of one of the tulips. I'll point it out to Odo. He'll know," she said with certainty.

"Okay, Brigitta," her mother said, moving towards the breakfast table and taking a small, thin piece of paper and pen out of the lone drawer. After a moment's consideration, Toos wrote a brief message she was sure Odo would understand. "No visitors this weekend," it said. Brigitta looked over her shoulder as she wrote, silently nodding her approval.

"When you give them the flowers, just tell them that we don't have enough for an extra meal and that Bert shouldn't come." Odo's son, Bert, was a school friend of Brigitta's older brother Albertus, and he often visited. The shortage of food was never surprising. Toos looked at Brigitta and Johannes and said, "Even if a soldier finds the note, it won't give anything away.

And the flowers will be a kind of apology." Her smile was resigned and apprehensive at the same time. It was all believable, but you wouldn't want the Germans looking into your affairs. "Let's hope it works and Papa gets the message," Toos said, more to herself than to the children.

Brigitta put her hand on her mother's arm and said with the confidence of an adult, "It will, Mama. I know it will." She slid the note from Toos's hand, once again taking charge. "We can't have it just sitting in the flowers. We need to hide it. Let me show you what I mean."

Brigitta folded the sheet of paper, already onion-skin thin, into a flattened cylinder, then held one of the tulips—the only red one—upside down between her knees. With tiny expert fingers, she slid it into the stem of the flower, curving it so that it quite naturally took the shape of the stalk. The tip of the paper jutted out just enough to be grasped and pulled out. "There," she said, under the admiring gaze of her mother and brother. "Papa showed me the last time he was home," she added quietly. "Odo knows this game. That's why I know it will work."

"Let's find a basket for them," said Toos, holding her voice steady, emotionless. Her daughter's cleverness moved her. Grabbing a tattered basket from the mudroom behind the kitchen, Toos returned to find Johannes and Brigitta arranging the flowers in a bundle and tying them with twine.

"Here, Mama," Brigitta said, holding out the bouquet, one hand beneath the flower heads, the other under the stems. Toos set the basket on the floor so Brigitta could place the flowers in it. She had put the red tulip on top. The paper could not be seen. Balancing the basket's handle over her arm, Brigitta looked from her mother to Johannes and said, "Let's go."

"Be careful," Toos warned them. "Walk along the canal. You're not likely to meet any soldiers there."

Brigitta nodded. She knew the best route. Walk south along the canal to the next bridge rather than take the one closest to their house. Walk near the water, not the road, as the soldiers tended not to go near the canals. Odo's house was on the other side, beside the church, two buildings south of the bridge.

As they walked, Johannes was silent, his earlier nervousness not apparent. He picked up stones, attempting to skip them on the water. Brigitta watched him, hoping they looked natural. It always seemed that when you wanted to look a certain way, you didn't, she thought. Did they seem suspicious? She tried not to think about it as she swung the basket with a carefree air.

When they reached the bridge, Brigitta felt a heady rush, that feeling of getting away with something. She noticed a German soldier a ways down the canal and tried not to walk any faster. She was glad that Johannes was still busy looking for rocks. He stopped briefly and gave her a look that let her know that he was paying full attention. He was nervous, stuttered, and was sometimes speechless, but he never missed a beat. Brigitta smiled at him and he winked.

They crossed the bridge together and walked down the other side of the canal, their footsteps hugging the turf at the water's edge. As they passed the church, Brigitta looked up for a moment at the steeple, then downstream, and saw that the soldier had walked farther south—farther away from them. She nodded her head in a discreet salute to the church tower and whispered a quick *danke**under her breath.

As they came up to Odo's house, they saw Bert and his mother, Katje, in the window, watching them. When Brigitta knocked at the door, it took Katje mere seconds to open it.

"Brigitta! Johannes! Come in! Why, you've brought flowers from your garden! How pretty!" Katje took the basket from her, immediately aware of Brigitta's index finger on the stem of the red tulip.

"Yes," she said. "Mama asked me to tell you that we haven't enough for an extra meal tomorrow, and that Bert should come another time. I hope the flowers make up for it a little bit." Brigitta spoke with a hint of embarrassment, always aware that someone might be listening.

"Oh, please don't worry. Tell your mother it doesn't matter. He'll go over another day." Katje, too, was well versed in the game. "Odo, come and see the flowers Brigitta brought us from her garden. The tulips are beautiful."

When Odo stepped into the vestibule, he smiled knowingly at Brigitta and Johannes and took the basket. "Thanks, Brigitta. Your flowers always brighten up a room. I see you weren't willing to give up your lemon elegance," he added with a smile, briefly touching the stem of the red tulip so that Brigitta could see.

"Not just yet," she answered. "And now we really must be going. The sun is going down. It'll be curfew soon enough."

"Run along, you two. We'll see you soon," Katje said, kissing Brigitta on the forehead and squeezing Johannes's shoulder.

Later that evening, after supper, Toos and the children sat quietly in the living room, waiting apprehensively. When Papa didn't arrive, they tumbled into their beds, exhausted. Brigitta's happiness at not seeing the person she loved best didn't strike her as odd. She fell asleep with a smile on her face.

85

Liberation in Nijmegen

No, I will not cry
I will not cry
I will not
The soldiers have let Mama cross the line
with the baby and Josef. Papa watches her
go, Martinus and I frantic. Shooting in the streets
flooded with running townspeople.
They get ahead
of me, tell me to wait under a portico. I don't listen,
scramble across the street after them as shots ring
out. No one spanks me, though I wait for it
No, I will not cry
I will not cry
I will not
Papa leaves us with neighbours, goes to
find Mama. We walk, we walk, end up in a garage outside
city limits, I've never been here before. We stop
for the night, along with many others but they have
parents with them
No, I will not cry
I will not cry
I will not
I don't know where our luggage went, we sleep on beds
in the basement, take turns sleeping across
the mattress to make room, eat biscuits and water

By Thursday, we are liberated, the city is free but no one
knows what to do with us. A man on a bike takes me to
my uncle's in Ubbergen, Martinus goes back to our house,
hoping to find Papa. Uncle Loek doesn't really want me
No, I will not cry
I will not cry
I will not
Later, I find out that Martinus and Papa met up, then found
Mama at the local dairy, her breasts had gone dry, she went

where the milk was. They had a reunion. I was the only
one missing
No I will not cry
I will not cry
I will not ...
But I do

Institut Henri Jaspar, Brussels

Peeling paint, narrow hallways
shadows run
on mint-green walls.
I peer into the stairwells
see smashed windows, shards of glass
on the landing.
In the bathroom, rows of sinks, some
hanging precariously, others with
broken pipes.
Here I washed my face.
Bathtub where I once soaked
now lined with rust, bottom coated
with dried sludge.

I arrived on 24 December 1944,
here, where the children of employees
from a prominent Belgian company used
to vacation—
now a hostel for young war refugees
from France, Holland, beyond.
We stripped, were checked for lice
(I had nits)
were given night clothes, shoes, uniforms,
were fattened up, weighed weekly, followed by doctors,
kept safe.

The war ended in May, the Red Cross
slow to send us home.
While we waited, we searched the forests, pretended
we were Girl Guides, played games of looking
for Hitler.

So much untold today by
the graffiti on the walls.

Chapter Three

The Survivors

Manna from Heaven

Today, margarine fell from Allied airplanes.
Last week, we got
one hundred grams of oil and two kilograms of barley flakes
from the Janssens,
a tin of milk
from the Vissers, and
half a loaf of dark bread
from the Altenas.
Just last night,
Marinus brought
two kilograms of barley
and Cas another
kilogram of oatmeal.
Bitter when we mix it
but we get a good-sized pancake.
With the borrowed milk,
we got to have a nice cup
of coffee substitute
last Sunday.

There's been an outbreak
of typhus,
some suffer from
hunger edema.
But us,
we are managing.

A Dutch Jew Looks at the Facts

Some say that in Belgium
the Jews had it easier than
in the Netherlands.
They say
it's because Belgium was
under German military rule
and the Netherlands had
a civil government that was
more corrupt.

But if we're honest,
the Germans persecuted the Jews
fanatically in both countries
with orders directly from Berlin:
anti-Jewish measures
in tandem here and there,
from the discharge of officials
to the introduction of the yellow star
to deportation.

If we're honest,
it's thanks to the Belgians,
who were less influenced by
German propaganda
than the Dutch—
less betrayal,
less anti-Semitism
(no NSB'ers),
a solidarity,
a will to do more,
though earlier liberation
and Queen Elizabeth's intervention
certainly helped.

I never returned to the Netherlands
because Belgium was my refuge—
became my home.

Real Estate Value

We had another house
in Drenthe.
My father had it built
before the war.
Found out later
the architect was an NSB'er
a Nazi sympathizer.

He sold it.

Riches to Rags

Those Germans
they stole themselves
      rich
We had to turn in
our shoes
our blankets
our horses
They commissioned
our homes and schools
slaughtered our pigs
ate our food
took our daughters
      and still they fell

Staas

During the war, just
before we married
he worked at a nursery where they
grew tomatoes; brought
fresh vegetables when we had
almost nothing.
He had a little white sailboat and
white teeth,
always brought flowers.
The girls swarmed around him.

He is ninety-three now
sits on the couch
cranes his neck when I speak to him
as though it will improve his hearing
holds his cane in front of him, always
at the ready

Teaching Kindergarten

Temporary job in Friesland. No
warning, police burst in during
storytime. They tell us
German soldiers rounded up
eleven villagers, shot them on the bridge,
the only access to the school. Keep the
children here, they say, till we can clear
the way. With trembling voices, we continue
reading to them, keep the real-life drama
outside the classroom and hope none of their
fathers lies there
bleeding

Accuracy

After the first moment
of jubilation,
we realized the Germans were not
going to give up the city
so easily.
We knew a bridge was wired
to be blown up
so they could stop the
Allied forces.
Young *onderduikers*
(saboteurs)
managed to cut the cables,
stop the explosion,
and Allies were able to
penetrate up to
Arnhem.
Years later
I saw the story dramatized
in Richard Attenborough's film
and picked out
what they got wrong

Thunder and Lightning

*Bliksem en donder**
bliksem en donder
she would cry as
the house shook beneath
flashes of light.

Bliksem en donder
would cry my old aunt,
sitting up in bed, startled
as bombers hissed
throughout the night.

I could not reason with her,
senility had tightened its hold
I could only take her tiny
fragile hand and tell her
everything would be all right.

The Department Store

At Vroom & Dreesmann*
where a tailor would sit sewing
fine garments
in a windowed atelier overlooking
the street,
there was a coating of fine dust
the absence of customers
a certain malaise.
During an air raid, the employees
sought refuge in the cellar and
stood in a foot of water
from the burst mains.
Rescuers slid a long pipe down
to send food and provisions,
but there was no digging equipment, no
way to get them out.
We heard the voices through the pipe,
wrought with desperation and fear.
Eventually there was silence.

No more Vroom & Dreesmann
Only a fine coating of dust—
        and echoes everywhere.

War's Insidious Bite

I

Nijmegen knocked to its knees.
Allied forces bomb the city centre
by mistake, a report later tells us.
Schools are hit, hundreds die,
more injured.
And Papa at home sick that day,
not on the train blown to bits.
Dr. Houtman not so lucky.
Told his wife and children to hide
in the basement:
they all died.
He had to live with the weight of this
misguided advice.

II

She gets through it, only to crash
into an army truck on her bicycle
at war's end.
Serious trauma, in a coma,
no identification,
a broken arm doctors don't set
because they don't know who she is,
don't think she'll make it anyway so
why bother?

Finally she is recognized by a nurse; they
fix her up.
When she regains consciousness
she's someone else,
never quite my mother—
constant pacing,

sobbing over clicking locks
and bicycle horns,
shrieking at loud noises,
pulling her hair out in clumps.

Altje, 1942

The few potatoes left have been harvested. The digging—oh, the digging! Altje's back is sore. And they're here again, the German soldiers, asking for water, for food, when they can barely feed themselves. What choice do we have? she wonders. Jakob is gone again, Lord knows what job he's doing now. There are so many Nazi sympathizers—you never know who you're talking to. So Jakob tells her nothing, to protect her and the children, Jaap, Aneke, and Ruud. She feels another baby coming—the signs that she's pregnant are there. Please, God, don't take another away, she prays. But is it any better to bring them into this war?

She hears the gravel crunch outside the window, the sound of footsteps. "*Frau*," calls the soldier. Altje looks up from the basin filled with water and potato scrubbings, sees the stark black uniform and hat before she sees the person wearing them. He could destroy her life in a split second.

"*Ja?*" she calls. She wipes her hands on the tattered flowered apron and walks over to the sill. She feels Aneke behind her, grabbing her skirt. Will the three-year-old poke her head out this time? Aneke is terrified but curious, fascinated by the German soldier, with his browned skin, white-blond hair, and stark blue eyes. She peeks around her mother's skirt. Altje is afraid of this soldier boy, too, and she doesn't want him to see Aneke—but at the same time, she doesn't want Aneke to be frightened. Though her daughter was born into this war, it hasn't made her tough. Altje can see the worry in her child's small freckled features, those lines shrouded by bright orange locks and serious brown eyes.

"*Das wasser, bitte*," the young officer says plainly.

Altje takes a glass from the makeshift shelving, pours water from the stone pitcher on the counter and holds it out to him.

"*Danke*," he says, taking the tumbler from her slightly trembling hand. He brings it to his lips with a sly smile that she catches before she drops her gaze. She doesn't let her eyes linger on his face. Jakob has warned her that such boldness can be viewed as impertinence and one never knows what will happen then.

"Mama, Mama!" she hears little Aneke cry, and feels her daughter's small cool hands under her skirts, on her thighs.

"Don't worry, I won't let things go badly for you," the soldier says in a crude mix of Dutch and German. "Your daughter is lovely. I know she is afraid of me. Please tell her I won't hurt her."

Altje slides her hand cautiously towards her daughter, until Aneke's fingers curl into hers, and then looks down at her, seeing only fear in her dark eyes. "It's fine," Altje tells her. "I think he means to be nice." Yet as she says this, she wants to pick Aneke up and run, hide her in a room and lock the door. She feels a sudden wave of panic, like a rising heat, imagines Jakob's rage at her behaviour, at this exchange with the enemy. Her face flushes as she tries to decide whether the soldier will make her pay later—and how—if she shows any sign of rudeness. She hangs on to outward calm.

Suddenly, Aneke steps forward, one hand still tangled in the fabric of Altje's apron. She looks at the soldier squarely, and he melts. Leaning over the sill, he extends his hand courteously with a soft "*Guten morgen*, pretty girl."

Aneke stands and stares at him, the look of terror mutating into a kind of quiet defiance. She doesn't take the proffered hand. After several seconds, she steps behind Altje once again, her fingers holding on to her waistband, but not so firmly now.

"Well ...," says the soldier, slowly withdrawing his hand. He sets the cup on the sill, his lips forming a tight, embarrassed smile. Thanking Altje once more, he leaves.

She bends to one knee and faces Aneke. The little girl puts her tiny hand against her mother's cheek, then wraps herself around her neck. Altje feels the stiffness go out of her small body as she leans into her. "It'll be okay, right Mama?" she asks. Yes, she tells her, yes.

Chapter Four

The Fighters

The Story Wasn't True

Couldn't be true,
I discovered later.
But it captured my imagination—
coins soldered to silverware,
Queen Wilhelmina's face
like garlic or a cross
warding off vampires
in another era—
supposed to deter German soldiers
from pillaging the cutlery.
The truth is,
some Dutchmen wore
teaspoons in their buttonholes,
showing the queen's portrait
as a form of protest.
But this was in 1938,
spoons produced
in honour of the fortieth anniversary
of her reign.
In the war years,
such spoons
were not amulets.
Such spoons
did not prevent
the pillaging.

Girl in a Flowered Dress
For Charlotte Schouten Escher, 1914–2011

All the things I have hidden in my
basket, wrapped around loaves of bread,
beneath fruits and vegetables. All the
things I have carried for the Resistance,
never once questioning.
This time, I carry a load heavier
than any basket of food.
This time there
is death in my basket, and I must unwrap it,
present it to his parents. Pregnant with our
baby kicking in my belly, I walk, I walk,
speaking the words over and over in my
head. I tell them
the bomb he was planting on the
railway line exploded in his hands. I tell
them it was noble, one for us against the
Germans, that he'd done the right thing.
But how,
in the face of their wretchedness,
and my fatherless child,
can I believe it?

I've walked all the way from Bennekom to Oegstgeest to tell them. Jan's poor parents learning of their son's death this way. I offer our baby, six months in my rounding belly, as consolation. A life for a life. But I know it is not enough.

The police are waiting there to take me to a prison in Arnhem. They are respectful and I am too filled with despair to be scared. I go with them, Jan's parents weeping at my leaving. They've lost a son and fear they will never see their grandchild come into the world.

I ride silently to the jail, feigning sleep so the officers cannot ask me questions. I don't know what will happen when I get there, and try to wipe my mind clear.

Four days, four endless days of hearings follow. They ask me the same questions over and over. How did I help plan to bomb the railway? What did I know about my husband's resistance work? What did I do to help?

I don't tell them about the weapons wrapped up in my basket, the newspapers that lined the bottom. I only tell them about the food I brought to hungry families. I tell them calmly, my voice never wavering. Even when they show me his burned clothes, I do not falter, as I rub my belly, look down absently at the baby's form, or beyond them at some random point on the wall. They cannot break me, no one can touch me there, no one can take what is left of Jan.

They tire of always hearing the same answers, of my blank expression. To them, I am just a stupid pregnant woman who knows nothing.

When they finally release me, I return to Jan's parents, show them their unborn grandchild.

The Namesake
For Heleen Massee-Schouten, 1943–

She went to Spain before the war
to help the partisans against Franco.
She was a nurse, worked underground with my
parents, was anti-Fascist, anti-Hitler,
and knew early on that things would
go badly. When she was taken by the
Germans, she killed herself in jail, took
a pill that was hidden in her hair, so the
story goes. Her name was
Jeane Heleen Schrijver and
she was my namesake.

Dear Folks, Love Ralph

Our Provost Corps dipped through Germany,
then into Holland again, well prepared for the
move, carrying signs that said, *This is Holland,*
a friendly country. Leave the cattle, on with the
battle, less looting, more shooting. They've fared
better here, farms well stocked; Jerries didn't take
all the spoils, so we can get fresh eggs in exchange
for cigarettes and chocolate. No reason to kill their
cows for sport, steal their meat when they are so
good to us, give us their best. They celebrate with
flags, wave at the troops passing by.
Country devoid of alcohol, all that's here is joy,
pure and simple. That's liberation for you. Don't
worry if you don't hear from me,
there's not so much to say but I'll write
when I can.

The Outline

The words were
written
inside the shape
of roughly traced
feet.
*Buy shoes for Klara
in this size*, he wrote.
Her toes are so cold.
Next day, I went to
Kresge's, did as he asked.
I boxed up the shoes
and sent them to his
host family in Holland,
and prayed for Klara
every night.

Homage to a Canadian Soldier

A gun repairman with a
French Canadian regiment, he
was essential, spoke English,
French, Yiddish, German, and,
soon enough, Dutch.

Now he speaks quietly, deliberately.
There are long silences
as he gathers, re-sees, reviews.

The memories are neatly filed;
he pulls them out, one by one
like stark black-and-white
prints, etched there
in his mind.
He gives them to me
without prejudice, tells me
about

the desecrated synagogues,
the farm animals, their bellies
bloated to two, three times
their size with malnutrition,
blown up by German soldiers
for fun,
the Polish labour camp he found near
Vilshofen during occupation
duty in Germany,
acrid smell of death in his nostrils
three hundred mere skeletons greeting his
regiment, left for dead among
rotting corpses at the end
of the war.

So many Jewish Canadian soldiers
went because they had to find and
kill that bastard, he said.

The rage is raw again, but
the years have dampened it.
He takes the stark black-and-
white images, stacks them
neatly, folds them into
memory.
His eyes glitter,
maybe with tears,
or, maybe just watering
with age.

Stationed in Veghel

Billeted with a Dutch family,
taught the daughters English,
they taught us Dutch. Fair,
equitable exchange.

German soldiers took their
milk, fresh produce
left them to
eat tulip bulbs, potato peels,
wear rags.

The mother wore a crisp white
blouse made from parachute panels
found in the fields.
The daughters darned socks from
the cords.
Even I pillaged.
Stole blankets from the barracks,
to keep my hosts warm.

The Soldier Watches Retribution

I watch them waiting in line, their
heads bowed as if in prayer. In some
places, the cost of collaboration is
death; in France, a swastika
painted on the shaved scalp.
Here, in a Groningen city square, the
moffenmeiden* shield their faces, await the
razor that clips close their locks, the
price for a German soldier boyfriend.
Some stand with already protruding
bellies, others wear broken hearts on their
sleeves. I understand the ways of love and
romance all too well, but as a Jew—never
persecuted but feeling it personally as I
help liberate occupied lands—I wonder
hard
at their choices

"What made you think it was okay to bring us there, Sarge?" Al asks Nick Watts, his sarcasm an attempt to mask his broken voice.

"Well, I wasn't wrong, was I? Are you going to tell me we should have left these people for dead? What the hell is wrong with you?" The sergeant's voice is tight, on the verge of cracking. But if it does, all the men will crumble—he's sure of it.

"He's right, Al. Just shut up. If you'd been one of those prisoners, you'd have been mighty glad to see us, so just shut the hell up." Dave's words are raw. Like everyone else, he can't quite clear his mind of the images from earlier that morning. Every time he closes his eyes, he sees their skeletal figures, skulls for faces with gaunt, hollow expressions, long devoid of hope.

"We'll never forget that, you know. It'll haunt us for the rest of our lives. I hope you realize that," Al says bitterly, dragging deeply on his cigarette.

Dave's patience snaps. He stands up, drags Al to his feet by the collar. "You little fuck," he hisses. "Is that what you're worried about? What about *them*? What'll *they* remember?"

Dave's eyes bulge with rage. His arm arcs in a low-slung swing that will catch the shorter man on the chin, but Nick is on him, yanking his arms back, shoving Al out of his reach.

"Enough! That's enough! Al, get off to your bunk. Davy, take a walk."

With fists balled, Dave takes his orders and walks. It's hell here, always with the same men, never a reprieve. He hates them and loves them—he's nowhere without them but wishes he was somewhere else. The fatigue in his bones is deep—the only respite he can look forward to is returning to the comfortable home of his billet in Holland. Mind racing, he pans through the day's events and realizes that investigating the appalling smell—at his sergeant's insistence—has made him feel better than anything he's done during this war: for once, they had helped with deep compassion rather than leave violence in their wake. Despite the horror of what they saw and the stench of rotting corpses, they'd rescued more than three hundred Polish prisoners from Łódź and the surrounding area.

Dave stops at the treeline, about two hundred metres from the German estate they'd commissioned as barracks. Hearing branches cracking underfoot behind him, he turns.

"Davy," Nick says quietly, falling in step beside the younger man. "Thanks for coming to my defence back there, but you shouldn't have lost your temper. Al didn't mean it."

"He was out of line, Sarge."

"Yes, he was, but these are exceptional circumstances and we all step out of line now and again. He was out of his head, couldn't help it, I don't think," Nick adds.

"He's right, though, isn't he? It *will* haunt us for the rest of our lives." Dave picks a stalk of field grass and uses his thumb and index finger to push the seeds up the stalk, just as he did when he was a young boy.

"Yes, I reckon it will," Nick sighs. He watches Dave catch the fat little kernels in his other hand and then crush them with his fingers. When Dave brings his fingers to his nostrils to savour the intensity of the odour, Nick is overcome by the simplicity of the gesture. He tries not to wonder if such simplicity is forever lost to him, clings to the idea that one day soon, he'll be at home again, watching his own son pick field grass with untouched innocence.

Afterword

The Complexity of Belonging

In her groundbreaking book of essays about belonging, *Losing North*, Canadian-born novelist Nancy Huston defines the French phrase *perdre le nord* ("to lose the north") as "to lose your head, to lose track," and even "to lose your marbles." The phrase takes some of its meaning from the geographical notion of finding "true north"—a point of reference that can help you find your way. And while society puts pressure on us to not lose our marbles, our way, our true north, Huston points out that it can happen when we simply leave our country of birth. She also says that leaving, much like abandonment, is akin to betrayal. Not surprisingly, then, Huston feels that she has betrayed Canada by leaving it, by marrying a French citizen, by choosing Paris as her home, by having and raising children there, and—most important—by choosing to write her many books in French.

A number of years ago, a close friend gave me Huston's book because she thought I would be able to relate to it—and she couldn't have been more right. I moved to Quebec from Ontario when most people were doing the reverse. Quebec's long history of nationalism and separatist views led to a mass exodus of Anglophones, particularly in the 1970s, '80s, and '90s. That exodus culminated with the 1995 referendum on separatism, which failed. Many questioned my move—particularly members of my extended family who had not spent much time in Quebec and were not intimately acquainted with its considerable charms. Given the often-heated political debate about Quebec's long-term desire for separation, it was difficult to explain to some what I quickly grew to love about my new home: warm, often politically passionate, cultured French- and English-speaking Quebecers with attitudes I respect, and, of course, a language I love and now get to speak every day. I like living in this in-between land of being neither French-speaking *pure laine* nor English-speaking Quebecer, but English-speaker-from-somewhere-else. It forces me to think about my own point of view in all this. Have I lost north? Am I without direction? No. In fact, the absence of direction, of north, has forced me to find what works for me. It's not north I'm seeking, but *my* north.

I've been thinking a great deal about my mother's north. Sometimes, I think she has no north. I think this is what happens after sixty years in your adopted country, of trying to assimilate but not really reflecting on it. What I mean is, she doesn't really think about why, as a Dutch immigrant, she might still be different, even after sixty years. The point is, she's here, and that's that.

When she went back to the Netherlands in the early and mid-'90s, however, it forced her to reflect and to reconcile. It made the chasm all too obvious and impossible to deny. Going back made her lose her north all over again. Yes, she found it again when she visited her aging relatives and got to speak their Dutch and feel bonded by a shared past. But she lost it—and lost it hard—when she met all their children and members of their extended families, whom she'd never known, and when she saw that their ideas and their Dutch were completely different from what she had known during her youth. On top of all this, she found an evolved and hyper-liberal country, one in which prostitution and marijuana were legal and the passing of the assisted-suicide bill was seriously on the table. So, she had thought she would find her north, but she found something else. Can you find partial north? Half north? What is that, anyway? Northeast by ten degrees? Northwest by less or more?

My questions about my mother's notion of north are compounded by something I didn't expect: the fact that when I went to the Netherlands myself in 2010 to visit her childhood residence, I felt more at home there than I have anywhere at any point in my life. I found my north even though I don't speak the language and have no close familial connections there. Just as I picked up and moved to Montreal, I could easily imagine moving to Amsterdam, uprooting my family and my life, and finding happiness in a shuttered, gabled house along one of the many canals. How can this be? My north clearly oscillates between Quebec and the Netherlands.

So what is north, really? Perhaps it is in some measure genetic. And perhaps it is also a matter of choice. But I believe it is also about tradition, even in the small things, passed down with little effort. To me, walking along the Prinsengracht and eating a freshly baked *speculaas*, the traditional Dutch spice biscuit, was akin to coming home—a home I had only known through my mother's will to share such food traditions as these cookies, New Year's doughnuts called *oliebollen*, meatball soup with nutmeg, Gouda cheese, and salty black licorice. These alongside Dutch terms of endearment, swear words, a love of gardening, the clichéd Delft Blue, and so much more. She may have lost her north after years of absence from her home country, but thanks to her, I have found mine—wherever it feels right.

Acknowledgements

This collection would not have been possible without the collaboration and assistance of several individuals and institutions.

Undertaken as a manuscript project in the Humber School for Writers' graduate program in creative writing, *Motherlode* benefited from the guidance of my mentor, Olive Senior, to whom I express my deepest gratitude.

I extend my warmest thanks to my editor at Wilfrid Laurier University Press, Lisa Quinn, whose belief in this project was palpable from the start. Her excellent guidance and enthusiasm were invaluable.

I am indebted to Marlene Kadar, the editor of Wilfrid Laurier University Press's Life Writing series, of which *Motherlode* is a part, who offered counsel, encouragement, and friendship during this endeavour.

My sincerest thanks go out to:

- The Dutch war children who told me their stories: Libby Boelen Emond, Carla Stapensea, and Kees Vanderheyden, whose contributions resulted in a significant part of this book. I would also like to thank Herman Ganzevoort of the University of Calgary and Peter Lowensteyn of the Canadian Association for the Advancement of Netherlandic Studies, who led me to them.

- Nico Hamme, a Dutch Jew living in Amsterdam, whose story of escape to Belgium through the Dutch underground network inspired me.
- David Kucer, a Canadian Jewish war veteran who told me of his experiences liberating Holland during World War II. Thanks also to his daughter, Susan Kucer, who made this connection possible.
- Pier Kuipers of Dublin, Ireland, who allowed me to use a letter written by his grandparents during the Dutch liberation as inspiration.
- Anna Massee, the owner of Het Grote Avontuur, a shop on the Haarlemmerstraat in the Jordaan district of Amsterdam, where we began a long conversation about her resistance-fighter grandparents, Charlotte Schouten Escher and Jan Willem Schouten. I am grateful to her for sharing their stories, both in Amsterdam and across the Atlantic.
- Robin Roger, who shared her father's wartime correspondence with me. Ralph Roger, né Rogow, was a Canadian infantry soldier who was billeted in Holland during the liberation.
- The dedicated and competent staff of several research institutions in Amsterdam: the Dutch Resistance Museum, the Netherlands Institute for War Documentation, and the Jewish Historical Museum. I extend particular gratitude to Anat Harel of the Jewish Historical Museum for her assistance in Amsterdam and with subsequent inquiries.
- Gordon van Wezel and his family, the current owners of my mother's childhood home, who welcomed me and showed me the legendary homestead.

Several individuals read the manuscript before publication and offered valuable commentary and support: Ginette Ledoux, Alicia Vandermeer, Michael Farry, Flora-Lee Bendit, Heather Mills, Steven Manners, Isabelle Laflèche, and Pauline Colwin.

I am grateful to Michael Carin, Robert Lecker, and Anne Lizotte for their advice and professional contributions. Special thanks go to Sara Rose Murphy for seeing this project through to the end.

My warm thanks go out to the following people for their inspiration and enthusiasm during this project: Jocelyne Alarie, Kathy Bouwheer, Annie Camus, Julie Faucher, Dawn Levy, Vicky Messier, Eric Schoeniger, and Jasmin Uhthoff.

In particular, I would like to thank my husband, Robert Kopersiewich, and my son, Eric, for their love and encouragement throughout this journey. Finally, I would like to thank my mother, Wilma Van Der Meer, for daring to confront her past.

Glossary of Dutch Terms

Bliksem en donder: lightning and thunder

danke: thank you

God in de Hemel: God in Heaven

Haarlemmerstraat: a shopping street in Amsterdam

Herengracht: one of Amsterdam's main canals, built in the seventeenth century

Hollandsche Schouwburg: Dutch Theatre; a theatre that the Nazis transformed into a deportation centre for Jews during World War II

Hoofdweg: Main Street

Ja: yes

Joden: Jews

Jodenbreestraat: Jewish Broad Street; a street in the centre of Amsterdam

Jordaan: a district in Amsterdam

kommen: coming

moffen: a derogatory term for Germans

moffenmeiden: Dutch women who had relationships with German occupiers

NSB'er: members of the Nationaal-Socialistische Beweging party, or National Socialist Movement, which aligned itself with the Nazi Party during occupation

onderduik: hiding period; a term used to describe Jews going into hiding in the Netherlands in the 1940s

onderduikers: saboteurs or underground/resistance fighters

Oudezijds Voorburgwal: a canal in Amsterdam, built in the fourteenth century

Prinsengracht: the fourth and longest canal in Amsterdam—"the Prince's Canal" in English—it was named after the Prince of Orange and has mainly residential buildings along it, most of which date back to the seventeenth century

Schiphol: the Netherland's main international airport

speculaas: popular Dutch spice cookies often in the shape of windmills

Spiegelgracht: a canal in the centre of Amsterdam, built in the sixteenth century

Stimpie Stampie: a type of *stamppot* (stew) served at the New Dorrius restaurant in Amsterdam

Vroom & Dreesmann: a chain of Dutch department stores founded in 1887 by Willem Vroom and Anton Dreesmann; there are currently more than sixty branches of V&D throughout the Netherlands

Westerkerk: a large, Renaissance-style Dutch Protestant church in central Amsterdam, built between 1920 and 1931

Zuid-Holland: South Holland

Books in the Life Writing Series
Published by Wilfrid Laurier University Press

Haven't Any News: Ruby's Letters from the Fifties edited by Edna Staebler with an Afterword by Marlene Kadar • 1995 / x + 165 pp. / ISBN 0-88920-248-6

"I Want to Join Your Club": Letters from Rural Children, 1900–1920 edited by Norah L. Lewis with a Preface by Neil Sutherland • 1996 / xii + 250 pp. (30 b&w photos) / ISBN 0-88920-260-5

And Peace Never Came by Elisabeth M. Raab with Historical Notes by Marlene Kadar • 1996 / x + 196 pp. (12 b&w photos, map) / ISBN 0-88920-281-8

Dear Editor and Friends: Letters from Rural Women of the North-West, 1900–1920 edited by Norah L. Lewis • 1998 / xvi + 166 pp. (20 b&w photos) / ISBN 0-88920-287-7

The Surprise of My Life: An Autobiography by Claire Drainie Taylor with a Foreword by Marlene Kadar • 1998 / xii + 268 pp. (8 colour photos and 92 b&w photos) / ISBN 0-88920-302-4

Memoirs from Away: A New Found Land Girlhood by Helen M. Buss / Margaret Clarke • 1998 / xvi + 153 pp. / ISBN 0-88920-350-4

The Life and Letters of Annie Leake Tuttle: Working for the Best by Marilyn Färdig Whiteley • 1999 / xviii + 150 pp. / ISBN 0-88920-330-x

Marian Engel's Notebooks: "Ah, mon cahier, écoute" edited by Christl Verduyn • 1999 / viii + 576 pp. / ISBN 0-88920-333-4 cloth / ISBN 0-88920-349-0 paper

Be Good Sweet Maid: The Trials of Dorothy Joudrie by Audrey Andrews • 1999 / vi + 276 pp. / ISBN 0-88920-334-2

Working in Women's Archives: Researching Women's Private Literature and Archival Documents edited by Helen M. Buss and Marlene Kadar • 2001 / vi + 120 pp. / ISBN 0-88920-341-5

Repossessing the World: Reading Memoirs by Contemporary Women by Helen M. Buss • 2002 / xxvi + 206 pp. / ISBN 0-88920-408-x cloth / ISBN 0-88920-410-1 paper

Chasing the Comet: A Scottish-Canadian Life by Patricia Koretchuk • 2002 / xx + 244 pp. / ISBN 0-88920-407-1

The Queen of Peace Room by Magie Dominic • 2002 / xii + 115 pp. / ISBN 0-88920-417-9

China Diary: The Life of Mary Austin Endicott by Shirley Jane Endicott • 2002 / xvi + 251 pp. / ISBN 0-88920-412-8

Broad Is the Way: Stories from Mayerthorpe by Margaret Norquay • 2008 / x + 106 pp. (6 b&w photos) / ISBN 978-1-55458-020-0

Becoming My Mother's Daughter: A Story of Survival and Renewal by Erika Gottlieb • 2008 / x + 178 pp. (36 b&w illus., 17 colour) / ISBN 978-1-55458-030-9

Leaving Fundamentalism: Personal Stories edited by G. Elijah Dann • 2008 / xii + 234 pp. / ISBN 978-1-55458-026-2

Bearing Witness: Living with Ovarian Cancer edited by Kathryn Carter and Lauri Elit • 2009 / viii + 94 pp. / ISBN 978-1-55458-055-2

Dead Woman Pickney: A Memoir of Childhood in Jamaica by Yvonne Shorter Brown • 2010 / viii + 202 pp. / ISBN 978-1-55458-189-4

I Have a Story to Tell You by Seemah C. Berson • 2010 / xx + 288 pp. (24 b&w photos) / ISBN 978-1-55458-219-8

We All Giggled: A Bourgeois Family Memoir by Thomas O. Hueglin • 2010 / xiv + 232 pp. (20 b&w photos) / ISBN 978-1-55458-262-4

Just a Larger Family: Letters of Marie Williamson from the Canadian Home Front, 1940–1944 edited by Mary F. Williamson and Tom Sharp • 2011 / xxiv + 378 pp. (16 b&w photos) / ISBN 978-1-55458-323-2

Burdens of Proof: Faith, Doubt, and Identity in Autobiography by Susanna Egan • 2011 / x + 200 pp. / ISBN 978-1-55458-333-1

Accident of Fate: A Personal Account 1938–1945 by Imre Rochlitz with Joseph Rochlitz • 2011 / xiv + 226 pp. (50 b&w photos, 5 maps) / ISBN 978-1-55458-267-9

The Green Sofa by Natascha Würzbach, translated by Raleigh Whitinger • 2012 / xiv + 240 pp. (5 b&w photos) / ISBN 978-1-55458-334-8

Unheard Of: Memoirs of a Canadian Composer by John Beckwith • 2012 / x + 393 pp. (74 illus., 8 musical examples) / ISBN 978-1-55458-358-4

Borrowed Tongues: Life Writing, Migration, and Translation by Eva C. Karpinski • 2012 / viii + 274 pp. / ISBN 978-1-55458-357-7

Basements and Attics, Closets and Cyberspace: Explorations in Canadian Women's Archives edited by Linda M. Morra and Jessica Schagerl • 2012 / x + 338 pp. / ISBN 978-1-55458-632-5

The Memory of Water by Allen Smutylo • 2013 / x + 262 pp. (65 colour illus.) / ISBN 978-1-55458-842-8

The Unwritten Diary of Israel Unger, Revised Edition by Carolyn Gammon and Israel Unger • 2013 / ix + 230 pp. (b&w illus.) / ISBN 978-1-77112-011-1

Boom! Manufacturing Memoir for the Popular Public by Julie Rak • 2013 / viii + 249 pp. (b&w illus.) / ISBN 978-1-55458-939-5

Motherlode: A Mosaic of Dutch Wartime Experience by Carolyne Van Der Meer • 2014 / xiv + 132 pp. (6 b&w photos) / ISBN 978-1-77112-005-0

Not the Whole Story: Challenging the Single Mother Narrative edited by Lea Caragata and Judit Alcalde • forthcoming 2014 / ISBN 978-1-55458-624-0